THE PRISON PROJECT

THE PRISON PROJECT

AIMEE FRIEL

The Book Guild

First published in Great Britain in 2026 by
The Book Guild Ltd
Unit E2 Airfield Business Park,
Harrison Road, Market Harborough,
Leicestershire. LE16 7UL
Tel: 0116 2792299
www.bookguild.co.uk
Email: info@bookguild.co.uk

The manufacturer's authorised representative in the EU
for product safety is Authorised Rep Compliance Ltd,
71 Lower Baggot Street, Dublin D02 P593 Ireland (www.arccompliance.com)

Typeset in 11pt Garamond Pro

Printed and bound in Great Britain by CMP UK

ISBN 978 1835744 000

British Library Cataloguing in Publication Data.
A catalogue record for this book is available from the British Library.

This book is dedicated to my gran, Mary Marthinsen,
and my mum, Debbie Friel.
Thank you for encouraging me to
follow my dreams and for believing in me.
I love you both so much.

A Note from the Author

This memoir is a true account of my time working in a prison. While the events are described as accurately as possible from my memory and perspective, the names of individuals have been changed and identifying features – such as physical appearances – have been altered or removed to protect their privacy. All individuals have been anonymised out of respect and confidentiality.

Trigger warning: this book contains references to drug and alcohol use, domestic violence, sexual abuse, adverse childhood experiences (ACEs), and trauma. This book contains strong language. It is not suitable for children.

Introduction

I taught dance in a Scottish prison, on and off, for several years. Yep, dance. In prison. My name is Aimee, and I'm probably the last person you'd expect to find behind bars. I'm twenty-nine years old, but back when I worked in the prison, I was much younger; in fact, in my first year there, I was only twenty-one – the same age as some of the inmates in my class. That was intimidating at first, but, like most things, I adjusted quickly.

I spent almost all of my twenties working as a full-time Dance Artist, and I loved it. I felt fulfilled, proud, and genuinely happy in my job. I was one of those rare and lucky people who didn't get the Sunday scaries. If anything, I was buzzing for Monday. Most of my work was in community settings: schools, additional support needs units, alternative education centres, and – of most relevance to this book – a prison.

After graduating from dance college, where I spent hours obsessing over pirouettes and performance pieces, I never imagined my first "big girl job" would involve banter with some of Scotland's most dangerous prisoners. Originally, I had my sights set on performance – maybe the West End or cruise ships. But while studying I started teaching dance on the side for a bit of extra pocket money (in other words, to fund my student nights out at Jelly Baby nightclub – RIP!). I also worked at the St. Enoch Shopping Centre, mopping floors and cleaning the food court. My twin sister and some pals worked there too, so, weirdly, I've got some fond memories of that time.

Looking back, I've no idea how I juggled it all. Dance training was intense – physically, mentally, emotionally. There was constant pressure to stay in shape, and, honestly, it felt like my worth depended on it. I'm sure a lot of other dancers have felt the same. Hopefully, the industry's changing for the better. Between classes, work, extra training, and the occasional nap (if I was lucky), I was always on the go. But over time, what started as a passion for dance turned into a passion for teaching. I loved lifting someone's mood, giving them something to look forward to, and seeing that spark when they learnt something new. The more I taught, the more I realised how dance could change lives – physically, yes, but also emotionally and socially. It could empower, heal, and bring joy.

So imagine my delight when I landed a full-time dance-teaching job with one of Scotland's leading dance companies – and imagine my surprise when it led me here, writing a book about prisoners. Now, I know this topic might raise some eyebrows. I get it. I had to keep an open mind when I was first asked to teach dance in a prison. I'd barely been out of college a few weeks, I hadn't had a proper boyfriend, or a girls' holiday, or even a full-time pay cheque yet. I was all roots, no branches. Walking into that prison on my first day, I must have looked like a deer in headlights. Some of the lads reminded me of the "neds" I'd avoided in high school – the ones who drank Buckfast on park benches and fought with the rival scheme's young team. I say this not to stereotype them but to be honest about what was going through my head at the time. I was quiet in school, with a small circle of friends and no clue how to relate to the boys standing in front of me. I'd had quite a shielded upbringing; I was brought up in a small town with little crime.

Confidence was key – and at first, I had to fake it. But somewhere along the line, it stopped being a front. I grew as a person… and I'd like to think the boys I taught did too. I occasionally refer to them as boys because some of them were so young. The prison project I worked on was aimed specifically at young offenders aged between eighteen to twenty-three years old. I was excited but also terrified. The prison project aimed to reduce antisocial and criminal behaviour through dance – and I loved that. It gave me a sense of purpose. My parents were understandably worried, but I felt drawn to the challenge, and I'm so glad I said yes. I'm not claiming to be an expert – far from it. But I can offer my experiences and, more importantly, the stories of the people I met. Working in the prison gave me the chance to connect with people I might never have crossed paths with, and now I want to give you the chance to meet them too. Their stories moved me – some to tears, others to full-on belly laughs. I knew I had to share them.

Of course, I've had my fair share of moral dilemmas over the years. But I've also learnt to empathise. After all, we all start life in the same way: as innocent children. So where did it go wrong for some of these young men? Could more have been done? Could better support have changed their paths? I'm not making excuses for unforgivable crimes, but I am asking questions. Because if we want things to change, we must understand the roots.

At first, I worried they wouldn't respect me – young, female, nervous. But oddly enough, they did. In fact, we had more in common than I expected. I used to get nervous butterflies every time I drove to the prison. Over time, I stopped seeing them as "prisoners" and started seeing them as people – flawed, funny, complex people. Yes, there were challenges. Getting buy-in was tough. Behaviour could be difficult. But the pay-off? Seeing someone grow, change, and find joy in movement… it was magic.

One day, I turned to my colleague and said, "These boys could be the stars of a comedy series. You couldn't make this stuff up." That's when I started keeping a journal – and that's what this book is.

Being a dance teacher shaped who I am today. Working in a prison helped me grow into a more grounded, compassionate version of myself. It opened my eyes to my own privilege, and it gave me a new kind of perspective. So, what can we do to make change? I don't have all the answers. But this book is my small contribution – a tool, if you're willing, to challenge assumptions and maybe offer new opportunities for those who need them most.

I like to think of myself as non-judgemental. But I've still made snap judgements I wasn't even aware of. The good news? I've been proven wrong, again and again. As my dad says, "Assumption is the mother of all fuck-ups."

We all have biases. Hopefully, these stories help us look a little closer – not just at others, but at ourselves.

1

Magic Mike

"I'll dance till a drop, darlin'!" These were the slurred words I heard, followed by a string of laughter, as I awkwardly rummaged through my notebook. I was trying to quickly read over my lesson plan before the rest of the boys joined us. I say boys, what I mean is young men. Young prisoners. It was my first day flying solo at a prison. I had been teaching dance there on and off for a few years but always alongside a more experienced tutor who would usually take the lead. Now I was the experienced tutor. I was ready. Well… I thought I was.

I peered around the space. We were in the performing arts room. It had a dance floor to the far left with huge speakers. The walls were dark, and there were no windows. The room was a decent size, I'd say around half the dimensions of a typical school gym hall. The room was used for all performing-arts activities, including drama and music. There was a small stage at the back of the room, with a huge drum kit on top. There were also colourful ukuleles and guitars hooked to the walls; they helped to brighten the place up a little. The guitars were a bit too easy to reach for my liking – I worried that they could be used as a weapon. There was a small, box-shaped office in the room, close to the door and attached to the rear wall. This office was where the prison officer would sit during the lesson. It had glass walls so he or she could keep an eye on us, just in case. Even though the glass walls allowed the officer to see what was going on, something about this barrier made me feel uneasy. I was a little nervous about being alone with the prisoners.

A few more young men entered the space. Some were dressed in navy; others were in bright orange. To my surprise, they weren't in orange jumpsuits like what they wear in the movies. They were in joggers and polo shirts. If they were wearing navy, it meant they had been sentenced; orange meant they were on remand, which means they were unconvicted prisoners. I felt knots in my stomach. I pushed them down and charged on, masking my apprehension. I put a lot of pressure on myself to do a good job. I really wanted the group to see me in a positive light and for them to enjoy my class. I was excited, so I tried to focus on that. The young men had signed up to take part; no one was forcing them to turn up. I silently reminded myself of this, keeping my nerves at bay.

We hadn't been allowed inside the prison (or anywhere for that matter) for around one year due to Covid restrictions. During this time, I had done a lot of reading and training on the arts in prisons. It was now 2021, and restrictions were starting to ease; I was ready to put my learning and my new-found passion to the test.

I introduced myself to the group, making small talk. I tried to get to know them a little before we started the lesson. Shortly after, we started the warm-up.

"I'll dance till a drop, ma darlin'!"

There he goes again, I thought, this time loudly, over the top of the music. His quirky movement matched his humorous tone; he went rogue and started doing his own rave style moves. I mean, fair play to him – improvisation is no easy task. I just wished he wouldn't do it while I was teaching the warm-up! I suppose he just let the music take him… who am I to judge really? His name was Brandon, but everyone called him Brandy. I was drawn to his unusual hairdo: random shapes and symbols were shaved into the sides of his head, one of which was a wonky circle that resembled a halo. I could only assume he had styled it himself, which was ironic to say the least. He had a strong Glaswegian accent, and when he spoke I noticed a few false and damaged teeth, black and yellow in colour.

Oh no… I realised that Brandy's unruly energy had rubbed off on the other eight boys. I looked around and half of them had taken it upon themselves to sit out. It was a new group I had never met before. I knew it was going to be tricky; I hadn't gained their trust or respect yet. With these types of groups, this is most certainly never handed over easily, but I didn't expect to lose them this fast. I didn't even have a chance to win them over with my fun fitness games and competitions. I didn't give up… I continued with the warm-up while calling over the boys who were now on strike, trying to entice them back in.

"Woohooo!"

Oh no, what is he doing now? I wondered. I didn't even

notice Brandy stripping! The other boys were howling with laughter as Brandy whipped his t-shirt round and round in the air like a lasso.

"Let's *Magic Mike* it up in here, darlin'!" Again, an eruption of laughter and chaos emerged.

I was too distracted by asking Brandy to put his clothes back on that I didn't notice one of the other boys, Adam, stealing my alarm! We were given an alarm for safety reasons when entering the prison. It had a red button that we were supposed to press if there was an emergency. If we pressed it, any nearby officers would come and help as quickly as possible. It could cause a lot of commotion if the alarm got into the wrong hands. I looked around the room at the madness – Brandy was doing some provocative stripper moves (well, that was the attempt), while Adam was running round with my alarm, half expecting me to chase him. Another boy named Stephen had taken it upon himself to start playing the drums. It felt as if I was in a room full of ADHD. I wasn't very good at handling it.

In this moment, I felt as if I'd hit rock bottom. I wondered how I got here. This was not what I had expected when I graduated from dance college with a BA (hons) degree in dance. I hoped that Brandy and some of the others wouldn't come back to the class after today. In my first impression, they were too disruptive and only wanted to cause trouble. My wish was eventually granted when the youth work team showed up (about bloody time). They escorted Brandy and some of the others back to the hall. They later informed me that those boys had come to the class high or drunk (most likely from homemade hooch or from whichever drugs were being smuggled in). They were not allowed down to activities under the influence of any banned substances. The officers must not have clicked on that day, until it was too late. Oh well, that gave me a sense of relief at least. It wasn't likely the boys were going to act that mental again if substance misuse was to blame. Thank goodness for that; the worst of it was over.

You can imagine my disappointment the following week when Mr Magic Mike himself showed up to the dance session. Despite his previous behaviour being explained through drugs or drink, I had still formed an opinion of him: he was a hindrance in the session, and he wouldn't last much longer before packing it in. I masked this opinion for some time. I put my professional hat on and, of course, treated everyone equally, with respect and kindness.

I found out quite a lot about the boys each week. We had a few tea-breaks where we got to know each other. I found out that Brandy was nineteen and, shockingly, had his first alcoholic drink at around eight years old, supplied by his dad. His mum died when he was younger – that explained the band on his wrist which carried a photograph of a middle-aged woman. I had noticed this a few weeks beforehand, but I didn't ask about it. He grew up in alternative education centres for children with behaviour difficulties and additional support needs. He told me a story about how he hit a teacher when he was in secondary school. The teacher had shamed him in front of the class. The only way he was taught in coping with such unpleasant emotion was through anger, hence the attack. When hearing this story, I tried my best not to judge or make any comments that could cause a reaction.

Instead, I simply asked, "What did your family do when they found out? Were you in a lot of trouble?"

Brandon laughed and explained, "Hell naw! Ma da was well proud."

While I awkwardly half smiled along with the others, seemingly unbothered on the outside, my insides were a different story. In my eyes, to be rewarded for something like that is an act of neglect. When most of us think back to when we were children, we often didn't question our parents' beliefs or values. We were too young to know any different. We hadn't gained the maturity, intelligence, or experience to see the world through a different lens other than the one that was being projected on to us. Hearing stories like these made me so grateful for my own childhood. I'm so grateful to have both parents still alive. I'm so grateful to have two parents who held me accountable as a child. They taught me right from wrong. They taught me how to deal with my emotions. They gave me love and nurture. Not everyone has this privilege, and from my experience this can be a contributor in how some young people end up in prison.

Several weeks had passed, and I soon realised that my pleasantries towards Brandy were no longer a mask. To my surprise, I genuinely liked him and looked forward to him being in the class. He was still pretty wild and sometimes got a little distracted. He was always hyper. But I was seeing a change in him for the better. He began to use his energy in a positive way. He always walked into the class with a jovial swagger and a massive smile to match.

He'd hold both hands up in the air and shout out, "It's dance day – yasss! Here we, here we, here we fucking go!"

He began having so much enthusiasm for the class and even told us how he had been practising the moves in his gaff.[1] He then began recruiting new members for us – we had our very own mascot! He would always swagger into the room with true *Magic Mike* energy (minus the stripping; thankfully he hadn't done this since that first mad week – phew).

"Number oot a ten?" he'd ask while pointing at me. It wasn't a question. If I said any less than twelve, I'd get heckled! It was always a good laugh when that happened.

This had recently become the new ritual for how we started the class. I would ask the same check-in question at the start and end of every session. I'd ask the participants: how do you feel on a scale of one to ten? One being the worst mood ever and ten being the best, or somewhere in between. Or, in Brandy 's case, a twelve out of ten. He was always a very firm twelve out of ten and expected nothing less from all of us.

One day, I asked, "Brandon, how are you the happiest person I've ever met? You're in prison and you seem a hell of a lot happier than many people I know on the outside."

He responded by saying, "I just think to myself, why be depressed? Wit's the point? It's just depressin' innit!"

You had to be there to understand, but this was a hilarious moment; I was in stitches. I think it was the way he said it in his comical tone alongside his distinctive slang. To this day, whenever I'm having a hard time or a bad day, I think of Brandy saying this and I start to laugh. If he can find joy despite his hardships, then there's no reason why

1 British slang, referring to a person's home. The men at the prison always referred to their prison cell as their gaff.

I can't. He had such a contagious, positive energy which brought a cheerful, lively atmosphere to the class. When you were around him, you couldn't help but smile or laugh. He was such a big personality that something felt missing when he wasn't there. I think we could all learn a thing or two from Brandy.

2

Poster Boy

"Rigged! It's rigged, am tellin' yeees. This is no' on!"

This teasing screech came from Kieran during a heated game of wacky races. Wacky races is a game in which the participants travel with a partner from one side of the room to the other, racing other teams. The way that they travel for each round is dictated by the tutor. For example, it could be a wheelbarrow position, a piggyback, or tied in a knot in some way. For this round, the round that Kieran was jokingly outraged at his loss, partners could only travel while connected with one another in a back-to-back shape.

"Kieran! You absolute cheat! You and Gary's backs were not close together at all. Fair's fair," I jokingly stated.

"Eh! Our backs were as close together as a nun's knees!"

It wasn't exactly the most respectful comparison, but in the moment, I couldn't help laughing at his quick wit.

Kieran was quite well spoken. He could turn the Glaswegian slang on when he wanted to, but he was very easy to understand and mostly quite polite. He struggled during the warm-ups.

I learnt more about Kieran on the tea break that day – he was such a gab! I found out that his dad was also in prison; they kept in touch through writing letters. He had quite a few half-brothers and sisters, but there seemed to be lots of falling out amongst them, and he didn't have a relationship with his mum. Kieran didn't go into the nitty gritty as to why; instead, he changed the subject to something more positive. He didn't even stop to take a breath in between stories. He revealed that he was heavily involved in the prison's drama programme, some people even called him "the poster boy of prison youth theatre". He then told me the story of how he met his girlfriend.

"It was in here we met, funnily enough. Aye, anno, tell me about it! That won't be the story we'll be tellin' our weans when they get older. We met here at the performing arts space, so we're just gonna tell the weans we met at a theatre. Ha! Technically it's true. Us boys were doing a drama show and so the lassie prisoners were allowed to come down and be our audience. I'd seen her about so a kinda knew who she was, so a gave her a cheeky wink and that. From there, she hit out wae all the cheesy chat-up lines. A remember her making us boys a cuppa. Then when I told her I don't take sugar, she was all, 'You're sweet enough, aren't you!' I tripped over on my way to get the tea and she said, 'Watch in case you fall for me…' Next thing a know, she's writing her prison number on the bathroom wall wae a sharpy. I used her prison number to get in touch through the prisoner letter-writing system. The rest is history."

Kieran had a huge smile on his face while reminiscing. He had a nice smile, and I noticed how his teeth were perfectly straight and a pearl shade of white. He said he didn't have much of a family growing up, so he was glad he had his own now. He was later released from prison at the same time as his girlfriend, so they got together and eventually had a son. Kieran never managed to stay out of prison for long, unfortunately.

He continued without taking a breath. "She's heavy psycho the now. Must be the hormones. She thinks am cheatin' on her... even when I'm locked up in here! Canny blame her, I suppose; she's always been a bit psycho. Probably 'cause of her upbringing – it was similar to mine. She's gotten a little better since we met. I think she just needed a little bit of love."

Later in the session, we decided to do some mind-mapping with the boys. We asked a series of questions on flipchart paper, which they could all express their views on through writing their answers or thoughts on the paper. We did this so that we could identify a shared area of passion, curiosity, or interest. We then hoped to use this as our theme for a creative dance. We were able to have these chats and be more creative with our process as we had been working with this group for several months at this point. We'd gained their trust, respect, and engagement. The question which fuelled the most thought-provoking discussion was, what would you change if you could change anything in the world? Kieran was the first to pipe in. He started talking about how he'd change the childcare system.

"I grew up in and out of secure units[2] and care. I honestly believe that's what made me destined for the jail. I was surrounded by no good. The only options for pals were in for murder and that. The more you'd hang about wae

2 Secure units – accommodation and education for children and young people who have been referred through the Children's Hearing System and/or the Criminal Justice System.

them, the more you started to act like them. You then start to see yourself as one of them, no different, no hope. This impacts how you're gonna behave and the trouble you're gonna get in. There were no positive influences in my life. No child should have to grow up like that."

Some of the others expressed how if they could change anything, it would be the discrimination against ex-cons. This spurred on some chat surrounding the opportunities that were available to them upon leaving prison.

One of the boys stated, "It's better in here than it is out there. You have a youth work team in here, life-skills classes, education sessions. We even have work parties."

Work parties allowed the prisoners to sign up for a particular job. For example, they could work at the barbers, learning to give haircuts to other inmates, or they could work in the laundry room, or some even worked as bricklayers. There were lots to choose from, and in return the prisoners would be given a small amount of money each week to spend on canteen options (such as snacks and shower gels). The youth work team arranged classes such as dance, drama and music for the boys. I even heard of some youth workers hosting well-being and mindfulness sessions.

From the way that the rest of the chat developed, I could tell that many of the young people who had been in and out of prison over the years craved the security and certainty of prison life upon being released. Many of the boys had grown up in secure units – this was their norm for as long as they could remember. They literally didn't know how to be in the real world. They didn't know how to cope with the unknown; no one had taught them.

Kieran explained, "When you're in here, you have all the

support you could think of. When you're released, you're left to it."

When I got home from the prison that evening, it was one of those nights where I couldn't leave work at work. I couldn't shake Kieran's comments of how he moulded into the bad influences he was surrounded by as a teen. It made me think of the famous Jim Rohn quote, "You are the average of the five people you spend the most time with." In Kieran's case, it was whether he liked it or not. He didn't get to choose these people; it was forced upon him. This is more common than we may realise. We can't choose the family we are born into. Think of all the children who grow up with emotionally or physically abusive parents. Think of the children who are raised by racist, homophobic, or misogynistic family members. What about the children who are brought up around crime, drugs, and alcohol misuse? I'm not saying that children growing up in these unfortunate circumstances are destined for the same outcome. However, I do think that the way we are raised and who we are surrounded by can change the way in which we see the world and certainly the way in which we see ourselves.

There are mixed opinions on the accuracy of this quote. I try to interpret the intention behind it to help me in my personal life. When I think about the relationships in my life, I often consider whether they are good for me. I sometimes ask myself:

Am I the best version of me when I'm with this person?

Do they bring out any toxic traits in me?

Do I find myself acting in a way that doesn't align with my values?

Can I be my true self around this person?

Do they make me feel safe and understood?

Do they inspire and support me?

Do they give me energy and make me feel better, or do they drain my energy and bring me down?

Imagine giving the younger Kieran these questions. Can you predict what his answers would be? Let's be honest, even a very emotionally mature teenager probably wouldn't have the life experience to consider these factors when it comes to forming friendships. This is even more difficult for a teenager growing up in secure care. Potentially, they could have no positive relationships or role models to compare their new friendships to. They may not know any different.

As humans, we are hardwired for connection. It's in our DNA. Think back to caveman times; we are naturally pack animals. Therefore, it's in our survival instinct to form bonds with other people. We'd often rather be around people who are bad news than to be alone. Even as grown adults, there seems to be such stigma around being alone. We see people going to the cinema or going for dinner alone. Many people automatically think it's a little weird, or they feel sorry for them. I will hold my hands up and admit that I was guilty of this mindset as a teenager. My views on this have now drastically changed; I wish the rest of the world with this opinion would change alongside me. I wish we looked at being alone as empowering and inspiring. I wish we thought, *wow, look at that badass out on a solo date. How inspirational. They must really love themselves; that's great.* I think we are getting to this mindset gradually. However, it's even more difficult for children and teens to think in this way. Not only do they have the human survival instinct of connecting with others, but they also have the added pressure of trying to fit in with those who are associated as cool or popular. This pressure means they may not stop to think about the quality of these friendships or the potential negative impact. Perhaps this habitual fear of being alone in the world is a contributor to why so many young prisoners don't stay out of prison for long.

3

Untamed

After a few days of overthinking around Kieran's childhood circumstances, I decided to take a leaf out of my own book and embrace some much-needed alone time that weekend. I was living in a small town on the outskirts of Glasgow in a one-bedroom flat, so I was no stranger to alone time. However, I did also have a fantastic group of gal pals that I'd usually reach out to. Despite this, I felt that I needed a little independent bad-bitch time to get my sparkle back.

You see, I had a situationship which wasn't serving me well. We were dating for a long time, but we weren't an official couple. I wanted nothing more than to be official… I was infatuated. I want to go back in time and give my younger self a slap to snap out of it; it's as if I was under some kind of trance where I was unable to spot the red flags. But I suppose our mistakes are what shape us, so I shouldn't be too hard on my younger self. Maybe if, at the time, I had asked myself some of those hard-hitting questions from the previous chapter, I could have saved myself a lot of heartbreak. *Can I be my true self around this person? Do they make me feel safe and understood?* If you were to ask me these questions then, I likely would have babbled on about how these things take time to grow, and it's the twenty-first century so it's OK to be unofficial… I would have made excuses about my relationship with red-flag man. Now, I suppose these points have some weight to them, but I believe that in true love (or even in friendship), you should always feel safe with someone, even in the early stages. I don't just mean physically safe, I mean emotionally safe too – safe to be vulnerable and honest and flawed. Hindsight is a wonderful thing. If I found it difficult to be honest with myself regarding my relationship as a grown-ass woman, how can we expect teenagers to come to terms with the virtue of their friendships?

So, in the spirit of self-love, I took myself on a solo date to Costa, and I brought my all-time favourite book with me – *Untamed* by Glennon Doyle. I had first listened to it as an audiobook during Covid; I loved it so much that I couldn't resist buying the hard copy and delving in any time I needed a bit of wisdom. It's a memoir about Glennon's divorce from her husband, but it's so much more than that. The book has many key themes, one of which centres around trusting our "knowing". Glennon speaks about struggling with the decision to leave or stay in her marriage. She asked her friends, the internet and the church, and everyone had a different opinion on what she should do. That's when she realised that if she couldn't please everyone, she might as well listen to her inner knowing and please herself. There are many more impactful themes in the book, such as feminism, social justice, motherhood and parenting, and freedom from conditioning.

I was excited. I couldn't remember the last time I picked up a book. My usual night-time routine consisted of going to the gym or seeing a friend, followed by binging multiple episodes of *Grey's Anatomy* on my couch. My weekends centred around red-flag man, as well as popping over to my parents' house for dinner or a cuppa. They were as expected: concerned about me working in the prison, even though I had explained countless times that most of the young men were only charged for petty crimes, such as stealing, drugs or fights. I wasn't trying to defend their crimes; I was simply pointing out that I was safer than they had anticipated. They didn't buy into it, so I'd usually keep prison chat under wraps.

As I walked down Buchanan Street, book in hand, I had the chance to people-watch – something I rarely did when out with another person. I was usually too focused on being present and a good listener for the company that I was with. It was nice to walk in silence; it felt peaceful. I noticed the bagpipers on the street and the tourists gawking at them, snapping up some photos for their Instagram stories. I watched the day-drinkers waddle out of O'Neil's and the groups of young, hip girl gangs dressed up for bottomless brunch. The town was bustling. I wondered how I would react if I ever bumped into an ex-prisoner in Glasgow city centre. Would I approach them? Would they approach me? Would it be awkward? What if they asked to keep in touch and wanted to add me on socials? How would I politely decline? What if they tried to stalk me?

My overthinking came to a halt when I arrived at the St Enoch Centre, my old place of work before I graduated from dance college. As I entered the shopping centre, I caught a whiff of the cleaning fumes, and it instantly took me back to my college days – mopping those car-park stairs at 7am every Saturday and Sunday. I strolled into Costa, feeling grateful that those days were behind me, ordered my usual caramel frap, and when it arrived, I eagerly got stuck into my book. Since I had read the book a few times, I flipped to a chapter that I felt would resonate with my current work situation: boys.

Although I had read this book before, it still captivated me as much as it had the very first time, probably more so now, because as I was reading, I was also taking mental notes, relating Glennon Doyle's insights to the young men I worked with at the prison. In this chapter, Glennon speaks about making a conscious effort to raise her daughters as feminists – telling them stories of brave, powerful women and having meaningful conversations about breaking the stereotypes of what it means to be a woman. Despite these efforts, Glennon realised that she mistakenly did not pour this same exertion into teaching her son what it means to be a man.

Throughout this chapter, Glennon identifies several fundamental life lessons she believes are essential for young boys as they grow up:

Men are allowed to experience the full range of human emotions, not only those society deems acceptable for them.

There is absolutely nothing wrong with being gay.

Women are not born to please men.

She had this epiphany while watching the news. She observed countless, horrifying stories: a young, gay middle-schooler hung himself after being bullied; a teenage shooter killed three other pupils in his school, one of which was a girl who did not have mutual feelings for him; and there was also a case of gang-rape committed by young boys in a lacrosse team. As Glennon watched these stories, she realised that they were the result of boys trying to comply with societal expectations of masculinity.

She explored these themes more deeply, emphasising that when boys are taught that strength means domination, they may cheat, lie, or manipulate to appear powerful. When they're raised to see girls as mirrors of their worth, rejection can feel like an attack on their masculinity. When they believe intimacy between men is shameful, they may direct that shame outwards as hostility towards gay men. When they are told that real men don't cry, their grief and hurt often harden into anger. When they learn that asking for help is weakness, they may suffer in silence rather than reach out for support.

As I read on, I instantly thought of Brandy. I remembered how he told me that he hit his teacher in secondary school after being publicly humiliated. "Boys who believe that men don't cry will become men who rage." These powerful words from the book stayed with me for the remainder of the weekend.

Before I knew it, the weekend was over. I found myself standing in the performing-arts space in the blink of an eye, listening to Brandy's mad antics which, begrudgingly, made me giggle. There were four young prisoners ready to get started, with Brandy last to arrive. He was escorted from a separate hall, which meant he arrived later. As Brandy walked into the room, I overheard the prison officer on shift poking fun at him for his striptease just a few months before.

"I'm rehabilitated now. Past is in the past, innit!" Brandy chirped back while holding his usual cheesy grin.

“Aye, because you’ve been spending time at gay bars?” the officer asked while holding a knowing smile. They seemed to have an inside joke, and I was intrigued, although I tried my best not to show it.

“Right, let me explain ma’self. I’ll tell the story to everyone. A wis fifteen and on the run—”

The officer interrupted, “You could have told them I was making it up and they probably would have believed you. You’re making it worse with an explanation.”

Brandy ignored the laughter and commentary and continued his story from the beginning. “A wis fifteen and on the run from that secure unit. A went on a bar crawl looking for ma da, knowing he’d be at the pub. He’s an alchy bastard after all. A was looking everywhere but couldn’t find him for the life of me! A walk by a gay bar – a dunno why but something made me turn ma heed and look in. And there was ma da… playing pool. There was a bouncer at the door so a wis tryna figure out how to get in with no ID. So, a tied my top up and over to make a crop top, like Britney Spears, and walked in like this…” Brandy mimicked his walk using a flamboyant strut, hand bent at the wrist and shaking his hips. The other boys couldn’t contain their laughter. “The bouncer let me walk right past him.”

“When you got to your dad, did you remain in character? And did he not ask what you were doing there?” I was invested in the story; I didn’t have it in me to not ask questions. I had changed a lot since I first started in the prison as a timid twenty-one-year-old.

Brandy didn’t respond with actual words; he just laughed. One of the other boys changed the subject, and with that, it was time to get down to business and start the class.

I wondered why Brandy was on the run from the secure unit. Was it really that bad, or was he just being a typical teenager? Maybe he just missed his family? I wondered how his dad responded to seeing him unexpectedly. These were all questions which I knew I would never ask. I didn't want to risk blurring the lines of professionalism, although realistically we were probably a little past that – I mean, he stripped in front of me a few months prior, for goodness' sake! Still, I didn't want to pry or bring up anything too deep; it wasn't my place. I thought back to Glennon Doyle's book I had read that past weekend. I wondered how Brandy seemed so comfortable in opposing societal pressures of what it means to be a stereotypical "manly man" in some ways, yet he struggled in other areas. He was so unafraid to come to dance class, to be bold and outgoing, to be extravagant and flashy, to tell a story of strutting into a gay bar. Yet, he would still occasionally come to class with a black eye and boast about his most recent fight. I knew that there was no simple answer to this question, but I certainly looked forward to edging closer to it.

4

We're All Just a Number

The following week, we continued with our mind-mapping during the last ten minutes of the session. This time, the question on the flipchart paper was, who am I? It didn't get much response. There were only two or three comments on the paper, opposed to the eight or nine we had a few weeks ago. Kieran wasn't there, which didn't help matters. He was at court instead. Brandy was also off. Apparently, he fell off the waggon and was back on all sorts of drugs. This worried me, more than I'd like to admit. I had grown quite fond of Brandon, and I missed his contagious energy. I didn't realise quite how much he lifted the others up until he was no longer there. I held the paper up to show some of the answers.

"12598," I read aloud.

"Yeah, that's my prison number," Stephen clarified. He must have noticed the confusion in my voice.

Stephen had been attending the dance project since day one. He was twenty-two; he'd been in and out of prison for a long time on short sentences. This seemed to earn him a fair bit of respect from the other young people. He never stayed out for long, and he had a quiet confidence about him; he didn't feel the need to act out like the others. He seemed quite mature in that way, since he wasn't easily swayed to be some sort of class clown. Most others would fall into that trap. He did occasionally hit out with some good one-liners, but it was always smooth and effortless. Stephen was around 5'9" or so and had a handsome but rugged appearance. He had a mop of bright-blond hair which he occasionally styled with a quiff, like Danny Zuko from *Grease*. Stephen's build was muscular and slim; you could tell that he was a regular gym-goer at first glance. I remember offering him a biscuit during a tea break once. He politely declined. He said he was trying to "get ripped". Meanwhile, all the others were scoffing five biscuits at once!

Stephen detected my uncertainty for a second time, so he declared, "We're all just a number in here."

There was a sadness in his tone, it gave me a strange feeling in the pit of my stomach. I didn't get the chance to comment. A prison officer entered the room and informed us that time was up. The boys said goodbye in their usual manner, in the form of a knuckle punch, and then they were gone.

Yet again, that evening I couldn't stop thinking about the comments on the mind map. Stephen's statement got me thinking about the importance of having a strong sense of self, especially when it comes to rehabilitation. This reminded me of a session a few weeks back. Stephen was the only one in attendance, for various reasons – Brandy was at court, Kieran was at the doctor's, Gary had a visit, and a few others had an exam down at education. Fortunately, at the time, I was working alongside my colleague and good friend, Sam. This contributed to a fuller atmosphere. We talked for quite a while, catching up as we hadn't seen him for some time.

When our topic of conversation came to a natural end, I asked, "So, Stephen, would you like to still take part today? I know we can't do our usual session since everyone is off, so would you like to do more of a fitness-based class instead? Totally up to you; no pressure. I know it might feel strange with no one else here, but we're up for it if you are."

Stephen mumbled something that I couldn't make out. He talked so fast and had a strong cockney accent; I often had to ask him to repeat himself. Sometimes it felt too awkward to do this, so in the past I nodded along, oblivious to what was being said half the time. However, I needed to know his answer in this situation so, unfortunately for me, that wasn't an option.

"Stephen, you're going to have to slow down. I don't know about Aimee, but I didn't catch a word of that." Sam saved me. I silently thanked her with my grateful smile.

Stephen slowed his speech. "I don't know. Yous decide. You're the teachers innit."

I glanced at Sam as we laughed. "Yes, but we're not going to make you do anything you don't want to do!"

"I dunno," he replied with an eased shrug of his shoulders. It took me a minute to realise, but he wasn't trying to be difficult; he genuinely wasn't sure.

"How do you not know if you want to take part?" Sam asked. "It's not a hard question!"

Stephen paused before answering. "I'm not used to making decisions. Everything is decided for you in here.

They decide when you eat, they decide what you eat, they decide when you shower and when you get fresh air. They decide when you leave the gaff."

I was speechless. After some back and forth, we went ahead with a short fitness session. It went well in the end with smiles all round. Even so, the earlier conversation left a mark within me.

I must admit, I had a soft spot for Stephen. There was a gentleness about him that sneaked out every so often. I could see it in his laugh and when his smile was genuine. I find it difficult to articulate my reasoning, but I had a good instinct about him. A few months prior, on the very first day of dance class, Stephen didn't turn up, even though he was on the register. We were told he was in the digger (aka solitary confinement). Apparently, he had attacked other prisoners and an officer, and they were rushed to hospital. OK, I know what you're thinking: my instincts were way off about him. However, I don't believe that to be true. It's moments like these where we could dig a little deeper. Instead of thinking, *what kind of person lashes out like that? Stay away from him*, I've tried to change my thinking to, *what happened to him?* Here's why…

"Come on, guys, shake what ya mamma gave ya!" Brandy announced at full volume as he entered the room. He knew how to make an entrance; I'll give him that. He went on to explain how he's finally sober and plans to stay that way. He was missing his performing arts activities too much, since he wasn't allowed down to take part under the influence. His enthusiasm towards the dance class was an incentive to stay clean. I was so happy to have him back, and the others seemed just as pleased. After a full-on morning of a cardio warm-up, partner fitness and a street-dance routine, it was time for a tea break. We got into some random topics of conversation, as per usual. Kieran was filling everyone in on his doctor's visit a few weeks ago. He was like an old man in a young person's body! He always had some sort of ache or pain, and he was very vocal about it in the dance class, making us all laugh.

Stephen joined in with the chat. "I hate doctors. I was banned from my last doctor's surgery."

Sam looked both shocked and curious. "What? Why?!"

Stephen answered, but once again too fast and with too much slang for us to understand. He repeated himself slowly. "The doctor stuck a needle in my arm with no warning. It was a reflex; I walloped him a good yin. I was in for my jags, yeah. But he could've given me a warning, innit. Couldn't help it."

Hearing Stephen's story made me wonder if his actions were a trauma response. My curiosity grew as our tea-break chat moved on to a different topic. We were discussing the best day trips to take in Scotland. The boys were sharing stories of where they've been and where they'd like to go upon being released. Someone brought up the Edinburgh Dungeons.

"I'm banned from there too," Stephen added.

We all stared with perplexed expressions, probing him to continue.

"One of the mad guys dressed up in those costumes came up behind me out of nowhere. I hit him away; it was an instinct reaction." He seemed detached from the severity of it.

The weeks passed and I noticed Stephen flinching a little whenever there was a loud, unexpected noise. I saw this on a few different occasions; no one else seemed to notice, probably because his bodily reaction was quite small. If they did notice, they wouldn't have said anything. No one wanted to mess with Stephen.

Stephen always kept himself to himself in the dance class. He never looked for trouble, he was always respectful and hardworking, and I felt safe around him – there was something about him that felt warm, kind and genuine. So, to me, the Stephen he described in his stories seemed like a completely different person. This thought inspired me to dig out some of my trauma research from the lockdown days.

During the Covid lockdowns, like everyone else, I had a lot of free time. I got bored easily – so I put this boredom to good use and undertook a lot of research which was relevant to my dance-teaching career. Below is an excerpt from my notepad where I wrote everything I learnt during this time.

Trauma

Trauma is an experience that is emotionally or physically dangerous or threatening.

It can be a single event or a series of experiences. What is traumatic to one person may not be to another. This is because we all have different personalities, upbringings, and life experiences. We each view the world through a unique lens. Therefore, we all have different levels of resilience and different ways of coping.

Humans inherently scan their environment for danger. For someone who has experienced trauma, this internal surveillance system is often heightened. This hyper-awareness can make it difficult to focus on tasks like learning or forming friendships.

The amygdala – the part of the brain responsible for processing emotions, is often compared to a smoke detector. Like most smoke detectors, it can be set off at the wrong time. A trauma response can be better understood by thinking of the amygdala as a smoke detector triggered by burnt toast.

For example, imagine someone was attacked in a forest as an infant and has no conscious memory of the event. Even if the person forgets, the amygdala remembers. It may now code forests as dangerous, causing a trauma response whenever that individual is near a forest. This can manifest as a fight, flight, or freeze response.

Dissociation is one form of the freeze response. It involves a disconnection from the body. Steve Haines explains this in his book – Trauma is Really Strange. He describes the experience of an explorer who was attacked by a lion: "It caused a sort of dreaminess in which there was no feeling of panic or terror."

People who experience dissociation often report feeling numb, or outside their body, like they're observing it rather than living in it. For this reason, many healthcare professionals recommend sensory and mindfulness-based activities to aid recovery.

Reading this part of my research reminded me of Stephen from the prison. He subconsciously interpreted the environment in his doctor's surgery and at the Edinburgh Dungeons as threatening. His brain likely processed this so quickly and automatically that he didn't have a chance to think it through.

As I read through my old notes, I realised that healing from trauma is about reconnecting with the body. That's one reason I advocate for dance lessons in prisons and secure units. If prisoners are given the resources to heal, they move closer to rehabilitation and desistance. Dance focuses on bodily awareness and breath. Learners engage with how movement feels, often using imagery to guide physical exploration. For example, to teach a contraction, a teacher might say, "Imagine being punched in the stomach, or draw your belly button towards your spine." Healing from trauma is about tuning into the body – and so is dance.

I felt inspired, and so I continued reading my old notes…

PTSD

Post-Traumatic Stress Disorder (PTSD) is an anxiety disorder triggered by a threatening event or series of events.

People with PTSD often endure flashbacks, nightmares, emotional numbing, or dissociation.

They may feel detached from others, and hypervigilance can lead to irritability, poor sleep, and difficulty concentrating.

Bessel Van Der Kolk, author of The Body Keeps the Score*, writes: "For every soldier who serves in a war zone abroad, there are ten children endangered in their own homes." He also argues that trauma from caregiver abuse and neglect is more complex and* *frequent, in comparison to trauma from accidents or natural disasters.*

Adverse Childhood Experiences (ACEs)

ACEs are stressful, potentially traumatic events which occur in childhood, before the age of eighteen.

These events include physical abuse, sexual abuse, emotional abuse, neglect, witnessing domestic violence, having a caregiver with a mental illness, growing up with someone who is incarcerated and growing up with someone who misused substances.

A 2015 study by Public Health Wales found that people with 4 or more ACEs were:

- *4 times more likely to be high-risk drinkers*
- *6 times more likely to smoke or experience teenage pregnancy*
- *11 times more likely to use cannabis*
- *14 times more likely to be a victim of violence*
- *15 times more likely to commit violence*
- *20 times more likely to have been incarcerated*

I often think about these studies when reflecting on the young men I've encountered in prison. I wonder how different their lives might have been had they experienced more positive early relationships and safer childhoods.

In the prison where I worked, the youth work team informally reported that most young men had experienced seven or more ACEs. This is not coincidental. ACEs are not only linked to incarceration but to long-term health, addiction, and social challenges.

We can't change their past, but we can try our best to better their future. We can also try to protect the young people within our communities from trauma. If we can't protect them from it, maybe we can help lessen its impact. So, the big question is, how can we make a difference? I'm hoping that the rest of this book sheds some light on this difficult question.

5

The Post-Lockdown Blues

After a heavy week trying to save the world, one dance class at a time, when Saturday rolled around, I decided to treat myself to a girlie catch up with some good friends from high school – Louise and her girlfriend, Heather. We decided to meet up at Sugo for some yummy pasta in the city centre, followed by equally delicious cocktails at Missoula.

We blethered on, reminiscing about high school, as well as chatting about our family lives and work stories. I loved my friends so much. The conversation always felt so easy with them. I could be my true self – chatting about my worries, my hopes and my dreams. In the blink of an eye, I had inhaled my pasta, and it was time to hit the road for some drinks – see what I mean about being my true self? I ate as if it was my last meal on earth due to a frequent case of feeling hangry.

By the time my first mojito arrived, I had already delved into my most recent prison story. I would talk about anything to distract from discussing my dating life. Things were still not great with red-flag man; I didn't want to admit it to myself, never mind to them. Honestly, it was really beginning to bring me down and affect me negatively. That as well as feeling lonely and generally struggling with my mental health. I struggled with living alone as a social butterfly by heart. I tried to be an independent boss bitch, but there was only so much alone time a girl could take. It was 2021, and some Covid restrictions were only just beginning to lift. This meant that we were finally able to go out and socialise more, so I hoped this would help. Although I knew that I could confide in my friends about this, I chose not to. I wasn't in the mood. Instead, I distracted myself by speaking about other people's problems… I spoke about Stephen from the prison, and how I couldn't picture him acting violently. I went on and on about how much I felt for him.

"I mean, what do we expect? This is what happens when people suffer from trauma. Hurt people hurt people," I preached, somewhat ignorantly.

"Yeah, I get that, gal, I do, but…" Louise innocently stopped me in my tracks. There was an awkward pause before she continued. "I've been hurt. I've experienced quite a few of those… ACEs, is it? But I've not wound up in the jail, have I?"

"Oh, I dunno about that; there's still time yet," Heather joked, hinting at an earlier conversation we had about Louise's obsession with Harry Styles – we often teased that she was close to stalker territory as a kid.

Despite the light-hearted comments and laughter from my pals, I instantly felt completely insensitive and unaware. Louise had been my friend since we were fifteen years old.

She was a true ray of sunshine in human form, the most bubbly, kind and happiest person I'd ever met, despite some major difficulties growing up. Her dad had died when she was a baby; soon after, her mum had developed an alcohol-addiction problem – she was a young mum who had Louise when she was only fifteen. She couldn't cope due to her alcoholism, so eventually Louise went to live with her mum's parents – Louise's gran and papa. Louise was raised by her gran and papa. They're wonderful people. Despite this, her childhood couldn't have been easy, with constant worrying about her mum. At the start of the year, Louise's mum passed away. Every time I thought of this, I felt deep sadness for my brave, beautiful friend. I admired her resilience and strength, and I wondered what contributed to her infectious, fabulous outlook on life. She always seemed so cheery and positive. If I could bundle up her optimism and sell it, I'd be rich, that's for sure. Talking to Louise made me wonder… Although trauma plays a huge part in why people are the way they are, should we be allowing it to excuse repeated poor behaviour? My time with Louise also left me feeling hopeful for the prisoners I worked with. If she could overcome her ACEs, maybe they could too.

Although I had a great Saturday, full of laughter and good food with my friends, by Sunday I still felt a lingering, sad feeling in the pit of my stomach. My mental health was taking a dip for some reason, and I couldn't figure out why. I also felt guilty for my low state, which didn't help matters. I told myself that I had no right to feel so down and that I was being ungrateful for the wonderful, privileged life I had, especially in comparison to some of the boys I worked with in the prison. I worried that there was something wrong with me, and I was concerned that this feeling couldn't budge.

This led to an overdue visit with my granny and grandpa, two of my favourite people in the world. I knew Granny would have some calming words of reassurance – she always did. I knew Grandpa would chime in too, comforting me and cracking jokes to put a smile on my face. They did exactly that.

6

Laughter Is the Best Medicine

A few months had passed, so Sam and I were building a great rapport with the boys. We were also building a great rapport with one another. Sam was around ten years older than me, but she still had the energy of a twenty-one-year-old. The boys facetiously complained that her warm-ups were too much for them. I, on the other hand, was grateful to get a good workout in during a workday. I was also grateful to work with someone who had much more teaching experience than me. I loved to learn and improve; I believe that the day you stop learning is the day you should call it quits. So I was thrilled to work with Sam. However, I didn't always feel this way, and I wasn't afraid to let her know.

"Sam, what did you think of me when we first met?" I asked this during our lunch break. As usual, we were at the café, across the road from the prison. We both had ordered our usual goat's cheese toastie with Irn Bru. Sam was obsessed with Irn Bru – so obsessed that someone from our company put a bottle of it in with her Secret Santa present one year.

"Ehhh, I don't really remember," Sam replied gently. We'd met around four years prior, but we'd never worked together until now.

"Lies!" I teased. "You never liked me; I could tell!"

Sam finally confessed, "Well, you didn't have a lot to say for yourself, did you?"

We both cracked up.

"I know I was shy, but that's only because you had a resting bitch face! I knew you didn't think much of me."

We both laughed it off and continued with this banter as we re-entered the prison car park. It's funny looking back at first impressions. Even though reflecting in this way is always light-hearted, it reminds me never to judge a book by its cover. Sam and I bounced off one another so well when we were teaching; our lessons always seemed to flow so nicely. We would plan our lessons together at the café every week. However, due to the nature of the young people we worked with, we had to be flexible with our plans. We often had to scrap the full plan at a moment's notice, thinking quickly on our feet. This could be down to many reasons: the energy in the room, behaviour issues, resistance to our idea, attendance, injury, the list goes on. Sometimes it felt as if we could read each other's minds in those time pressured moments. We felt very in sync while devising a last-minute Plan B.

Lesson planning wasn't the only thing we liked to do during our café lunch breaks. We loved a good chinwag, as we'd become great friends. Sam was like a big sister to me. She'd give me dating advice and listen to my complaints about family tiffs. She'd tell me stories of how she went travelling in her twenties and how she met her husband. She'd often FaceTime her husband during our lunch breaks. That was Sam's thing: she loved FaceTime. She'd flip the camera round to record me so I could give him a wave hello. I remember he once called us "the dream team". If you told me this back when we first met, I'm not sure if I would have believed you.

We finally arrived at the performing-arts space; it was a long walk from reception. The boys had beat us to it – the officers must have got through their drop-offs slightly earlier than usual. Either that or Sam and I had spent too much time dilly-dallying. Probably the latter, I know. During our walk through the prison, Sam was still agonising over my "resting bitch face" comment. She wanted more specific examples of her resting-bitch-face behaviour. We were laughing so much.

We had a full house, so fortunately a Plan B wasn't needed. We began the session with our usual check-in, warm-up, and creative game, before moving onto a contemporary dance.

"Oooft, Aimee, hate to break it to you, but you're going to have to start counting your steps," Stephen stated boldly during a partner-work section of the dance.

"Oi, enough of that, you. Aimee's a tank," Sam defended me. But we knew there was no need; it had become a running joke.

Stephen's partner for the contemporary dance was a no-show, so he was stuck lifting me. He mockingly complained I was too heavy, and I took the bait. I wasn't overweight in the slightest; that's probably why he teased. He knew it wasn't going to hurt my feelings.

After our contemporary-dance practice, we formed a freestyle circle. This was where everyone could take a turn of going into the middle to show off their best moves. Sam played some old-school 2000s R&B which got everyone dad-dancing on the sidelines. Kieran entered first. He strutted into the middle, with his hands in fists, across from his stomach, as if he was pushing a shopping trolley. He then mimicked taking items from the imaginary shelves and placed them in his make-believe trolly. He did this while bouncing along to the music in a carefree manner. You had to be there, but it was hilarious! Brandy went in and showed us the worm, along with some moves he had remembered from our street-dance routine. I almost expected him to show us his *Magic Mike* moves from week one. I was glad those days were gone! Stephen was the dark horse. He looked like a proper b-boy; he was fantastic! He performed windmills, 6-steps and freezes, all forms of complex floor work that breakdancers execute with great skill. He later revealed how he learnt those moves when he was "a wee guy" and that he was inspired by the *Step Up* films.

A few weeks passed, and Stephen hadn't made an appearance to any of the sessions. This wasn't like him; I knew how much he enjoyed the classes. I reached out by sending him a letter via the email-a-prisoner website. I wanted to let him know about a breakdance masterclass that was happening in the next few weeks. I didn't want him to miss out, as I knew it would be right up his street.

He replied with this:

Hiya, just had a lot on my mind. My mood's like the sun... when it sets, things get dark for a while but sooner or later it's gonna rise again and I need to keep that in mind but it's hard to see in the dark. I've been spending a lot of time with the dogs. I volunteer to help train the prison dogs. I talk to them sometimes cause they can't speak so they don't get all judgemental... unless your holding back on the dog treats. Apparently, that's not an issue for me. According to the staff that work with the dogs, I overfeed them. In my defence, I've tried the food they feed them and it's absolutely stinkin, so I make sure to sneak in some human food too.

I'll be there this week and next, it's good you and Sam are gonna take part too (gotta lead by example and all that).

-Stephen

Stephen stayed true to his word and returned to dance for the next class. However, his melancholy silence implied that something was still off. When he finally broke this silence, he started chatting about how he was being released soon. I wondered if he was worried about leaving prison and returning to normal life.

"So, are you gonna stay out of trouble this time? You gonna stay out of prison for good?" Sam asked softly.

Stephen shrugged. "Yeah, we'll see. If I can get away from here maybe. I have a better chance of staying away from bad shit if I move back down south."

"Ahh, I see. Are there too many people over this way that will get you into bother then?" I wondered aloud.

"Yeah, that's right. But saying that, even if I move down south, I know what I'm like. I can't keep blaming other people. It's only a matter of time innit."

I had that funny feeling in the pit of my stomach again. I wished there was something more we could do to help him. I silently reminded myself that we can't save everyone; they must want to save themselves first.

I thought about this some more in the days that followed. I was passionate about using the arts to help with rehabilitation and desistance from crime. Still, I had to accept that there may be inmates who were too far gone. Does this mean that the arts lose their value in prison settings? Absolutely not. Even if some of these young people cannot be rehabilitated, they are still human. They deserve the benefits that the arts have to offer. They deserve for their mental and physical health to be taken care of. They deserve to learn new skills and to keep their minds busy. They deserve to meet new people, especially tutors from outside the prison. I imagine that having positive connections with non-prisoners has a positive impact on how the inmates see themselves.

I've had moments where I've looked around at everyone during the class and I've noticed that every single person is laughing or smiling in the sincerest way. Not the fake laughter that we do as adults to be polite. I'm talking about good-for-the-soul, childlike laughter. I think everyone deserves to experience that, even into adulthood. I recently listened to a podcast called *Wellness with Ella*. In one episode, the host, Ella, speaks to an author named Naomi Bagdonas. They speak about the benefits of laugher, one of which includes increased creativity due to laughter lowering our cortisol levels. Cortisol is the body's main stress hormone, so lowering this is especially important for those who have experienced trauma or ACEs. Lowering cortisol can improve emotional regulation and physical symptoms of stress (such as heart rate, sleep and concentration). In the podcast, they discussed how laughter can have the same effect as a runner's high, as dopamine and endorphins are released. During a battle against addiction, it's important to replace the substance highs with natural highs. Who knew that laughter would be so beneficial in this way?

Next, they revealed how the people who we laugh with are those who we will have a more positive memory of – we have a deeper trust and bond with these people. So, it seems that laughter is a pivotal part of mental well-being, creativity, and quality connections. Think about most prison films or documentaries – how often do you see genuine laughter or wholesome friendships? I know that there is light-hearted prison content out there, but from my experience, it seems less common. I have only consumed light-hearted prison content through reading my own work. That's because it's from my perspective, though; I'm not too naive to realise that. I've only seen the laughter and joy from prisoners in the dance class. I haven't seen what it's like for the other twenty-three hours of their day. Our dance class may have been the only moment in the whole week that these participants experienced any form of laughter or happiness. Sometimes when I was having a low week, it would be one of the only times where I'd experience a good tummy-ache laugh. I noticed that my mental health seemed better on the days I taught dance in the prison. If I was feeling this shift in well-being even when I had a pretty good life on the outside, can you imagine how this shift in mental health would have felt for the young prisoners?

7

Toxic Masculinity

"Ha! Sam, you've got to see this!" I pushed over the equality forms that we had the young people fill out several weeks ago. We were on our lunch break at the usual spot. It was Stephen's last day, so we wanted to read over the forms to make sure he hadn't left anything blank. The paper firstly asked about the participants' relationship status. Options were in a tick-box format, ranging from single, prefer not to say, married, civil partnership, divorced, to widowed. Stephen had ticked the box next to single, adding in his own commentary alongside it so it read, *Single… as fuck*. A later question asked, *What do you want to get out of the dance class?* Stephen answered, *To get ripped. To be a machine!* While others answered, *For the sex appeal* or *To be a god in the club*. We had quite a laugh that lunchtime.

We returned to the prison, leaving our mobile phones and other personal items in the car. Like so many others, the prison looked like a college building. It didn't look old, or dingy, or run-down – quite the opposite. We headed to the front desk where we went through the usual weekly process to be granted access. We each handed over our driving licence as our form of ID. We both got a visitor pass in exchange. We placed our tote bags and jackets in a small box and onto the conveyer belt where our items got scanned. The staff checked the results on the screen to make sure we weren't attempting to bring in any prohibited items. This usually went smoothly, but there had been occasions in the past where our bags got searched thoroughly. The prison officers wore white shirts which had SPS (Scottish Prison Service) written in small writing. The female prison officers always had their hair tied back. I heard they weren't allowed to wear it down. I wondered if this was due to safety, to avoid a hair-pull attack from prisoners maybe? Next, we walked through the body scanner before collecting our things. The full experience reminded me of airport security. I remember years ago, when I first started working in the prison, I found this so nerve-wracking. I always had knots in my stomach.

From there, we collected our safety alarms and headed through several doors. We had to press the buzzer at each locked door and wait for entry. There was a little camera and speaker at all the doors; sometimes we'd get asked to hold up our visitor passes to the camera. They often unlocked the doors for us immediately, so we didn't have to do this. It was a different experience every time, depending on the staff. Back in the day, I found it majorly confusing to remember which doors to enter and which route to take. I would be proud of myself for not getting lost on the days I was teaching alone. I know this sounds ridiculous, but that is how bad my sense of direction was!

It was a long walk. The corridors were narrow with a lot of twists and turns. We passed many prison officers on route; most gave us a friendly smile or a knowing nod. There were also a few inmates who walked by. Most were accompanied by a prison officer. However, to my surprise, there were also some who were not. I didn't realise they were prisoners at first because they were wearing green. I hadn't seen this before. I later found out that green was for the prisoners who were in the industrial cleaners' work party. Most prisoners who landed this gig were open-side prisoners. These were the young people who were highly trusted due to excellent behaviour, therefore they were allocated more freedom within the building. A tall, young man in a green polo shirt walked by before turning back around.

"Oi! I know yous!"

I was a bit confused at first, as I didn't recognise him. *Surely, I'd remember if he'd attended one of our dance sessions,* I thought.

"From the TV… Channel 21. Yous are the two mad yins dancing aboot on Channel 21, aren't yees?" he asked.

Sam and I burst out laughing. We couldn't believe that all these months had passed and the prison continued to play our lockdown dance tutorials. Around a year beforehand, we had filmed ourselves teaching short dance and fitness classes. They were around twenty to thirty minutes long. We weren't allowed inside the prison due to Covid restrictions, so it was the only way we could reach the young people. This seemed like a lifetime ago.

When we arrived at the performing-arts space, we were greeted by a prison officer named Stewart. He was covering the designated performing arts officer who was on annual leave at the time. Stewart was only a few inches taller than me, with tanned skin and dark-brown hair, although he looked mostly bald. If I had to guess, I'd say he was in his fifties, around the same age as my parents at the time, or slightly older maybe. He had a Dundonian accent and seemed a little intimidating at first glance; he wasn't the smiley type. I'd met him a few times briefly, so I quickly remembered that this first impression wasn't accurate at all. I began making small talk as a result. I asked where in the prison he was usually based. He explained that he was involved in peer mentoring.

"I've heard some of the boys talk about that, but what exactly is it?" I asked politely.

"Well, it's in the name really. We get the open-side boys to welcome the new prisoners and to show them around. We allocate each new boy with a mentor, someone to look out for them, to reassure them. But there's more to it than that. We teach the boys about empathy."

My face lit up. I was beaming. "Wow, that's absolutely amazing." My enthusiasm was genuine. "I'm so impressed and relieved that you teach this. I read a lot of Brené Brown's research – have you heard of her?"

"No, I don't think so, but her name does ring a bell."

"She's great; I've learnt a lot. In a few of her books, she talks about the difference between empathy and sympathy."

"Alright, go on then. What's the difference?" I could tell by his playful tone that he didn't expect me to know the answer.

"Well, sympathy is when you feel sorry for someone. Empathy is when you feel *with* them," I clarified meekly. I suddenly felt put on the spot and unsure of myself. I could feel that my cheeks were flushed as my face heated up.

"Give me more than that. You're on to something."

"So, I think sympathy is when you try to look for the silver lining in someone's difficult situation without properly taking the time to acknowledge what they're going through. It's just brushing them off really. Sympathy is responding to someone's pain by saying, 'Oh I feel bad for you. But at least… blah blah blah.' I think empathy is when you are choosing to deeply imagine what that person must be feeling. To imagine it, you've got to remember a similar emotion that you've experienced yourself. It can feel vulnerable and difficult to do that."

Stewart nodded. He didn't get a chance to say much; we were interrupted by the participants walking in. It didn't matter though; I could tell by his demeanour that he was impressed. *Yass*, I thought to myself, *Brené would be proud!*

"Shake what ya mamma gave ya!" Brandon proclaimed at full volume as he entered the room. I noticed that his hair was styled slightly differently this week. He had a huge lightning bolt shaved onto the side of his head. He also had black bruising around his eye, which was extremely bloodshot. I found it difficult to look at him without wincing.

"Number oot a ten?" he asked everyone with his usual comical routine until Sam and I took over.

Sam filled the boys in on our encounter with the prisoner in the green polo shirt. "We had our five minutes of fame this morning. We were recognised on our way here as the Channel 21 girls. We feel like celebrities!"

"Aw, aye? That was you? I've tried your videos as well then!" Kieran seemed pleasantly surprised.

"Were you out your face on gear or something?" Stephen added with his Londoner accent. "I remember watching

Sam's rave one and thinking, *she's out her tree.* No one is that happy and energetic naturally. You was goin' for it, you were."

I burst out laughing at poor Sam's expense.

"No, I swear! I don't do drugs!" she defended herself while laughing her head off. The boys continued to take the mick until we eventually started the lesson.

We led a follow-on fitness warm-up, tailed by a game of sticky shapes. This game involved moving around the space in creative ways and making exciting, connected shapes with a partner, using a variety of body parts and levels. When the music stopped, the players had to make their shapes as quickly as possible. Winners were chosen in each round for the fastest and for the most creative. We used this game to get the young men used to safe touch and, of course, to improve teamwork. The competitive element of the game masked the vulnerability of trusting a partner. The game was quick-paced, so it didn't give participants much time to think. This meant they didn't get too embarrassed by being unusually close to their partner's body. This was important for some more than others. Especially Gary.

Gary had been attending the dance sessions since the start of the project. I remember his first day of dance: he laughed the whole way through the class. It was the kind of laugh that's used to mask utter embarrassment and self-consciousness. Then, when it came to partner fitness competitions, he refused to touch his partner's legs during an ab set of leg raises. Thankfully, his partner didn't make a big deal of it, carrying on without his support. But I do remember thinking it was a bit strange. I also remember thinking that we had our work cut out for us… I wasn't wrong.

After sticky shapes, we moved on to our jump-style routine. The boys got majorly hyped up when the music played, especially Brandy and Kieran. They were singing along to Scooter's "Jumping All Over the World" while simultaneously attempting to master the complex jumps, turns, kicks, and twists involved in the sequence. I couldn't help but laugh.

"Are you always this buzzing? Do you always wake up in a good mood?" I asked during break time. I looked at Brandy's black eye while squirming slightly. I was baffled that his positivity hadn't taken a hit.

"Aye, sweetheart. A bounce out of bed like this!" Brandy answered while mimicking how he would sit up from a laid-down position with a huge, cheesy smile on his face. "I'm even this happy when kicking wee cunts' heads in."

"Right, that's enough; we don't want to hear about that," Sam interjected.

"Sorry, sorry!" Brandy replied jokingly while holding both hands up innocently. "Dinnae mean to offend you, ladies," he added before changing the subject.

It didn't take Gary long to change the subject back again. He seemed to be making a habit of this around that time. He was always showing off by talking about the fights he was getting in to. Gary was muscular, slim, and quite tall. He was covered in tattoos; he had a sleeve and some more on his neck. He also had a letter tattooed below each knuckle on his hands. When linked together, it read *Piss Off* (how charming). He had very short, ginger hair and dark eyes. He made intense eye contact with me occasionally. This made me feel quite uncomfortable, as did his unfortunate chat-up lines.

The conversation took a natural turn; we were now discussing what everyone was watching on TV. I jumped in and told the boys how I had been crying my eyes out at an episode of *Grey's Anatomy* the night before.

"I don't cry. I can't remember the last time I cried," Kieran explained. This was in a frank, honest tone. I could tell he was simply speaking his mind rather than trying to appear as tough. "I don't get upset; I just get mad angry," he added.

"I can't imagine you like that. You always seem so chilled and happy," I responded courteously. What I said was only half true; I could, in fact, imagine him as angry… I mean, he was incarcerated for a reason.

"No, I'm like a different person when I get mad. It's not good." He seemed a little numb while explaining.

"When I was a wee guy, if I ever cried, ma da would gee me in trouble and tell me to toughen the fuck up," Brandon jumped in, in his usual light-hearted tone. "That's how a ended up kicking cunts' heads in."

"Listen, guys. Crying doesn't make you any less of a man. We're all human and it's a normal emotional response. We're conditioned from society to believe that crying makes you weak or less manly, but that's not true; it's totally wrong."

I tried to say this in a casual manner so I didn't come off as preachy. To my surprise, the boys were nodding along and listening without interrupting. They were usually quite bad for talking over Sam and me. Not in a spiteful way; usually it was because they were excited. Either that or those with ADHD had sold their meds instead of taking them. But no interrupting today. They were hanging on my every word.

"You've all recognised it yourself, but the fighting happens because you don't know any other way to express challenging emotions. You wouldn't dare cry or get upset, so the only alternative is anger. You also probably think it's the macho thing to do. It's not. I don't think it's attractive at all. It's these conditioned thoughts that get you into trouble."

We continued with the rest of the session in good spirits. When the class was over, we walked down the corridor with the participants and Stewart, the prison officer. Stewart was escorting them back to their gaffs. Before parting ways, the rest of the boys carried on, but Stephen stayed back to say goodbye. This was the last time we were ever going to see him. Even if he ended up back in prison again, he wouldn't meet the age requirements to attend our young offender dance classes. So we knew this truly was goodbye. It was an odd, bittersweet moment. I was incredibly happy for him, but I also knew we would miss him loads.

"Stephen, it really has been a pleasure to know you. We've loved getting to know you better each week, and we'll really miss you in the class. Take care." I gave him a tight squeeze. I hoped he knew how much I meant what I said.

Sam also gave him a hug. "We want you to have a good life! Please stay out of trouble. We'll be thinking of you and wondering how you're getting on."

Some wolf-whistling from afar interrupted our wholesome farewell.

"Gaun yersel, Stephen!" an inmate we'd never met before called out after us, praising Stephen for all the female attention.

Thankfully, Stephen didn't give it any notice. He thanked us for everything and gave us that rare but earnest smile. Then he was gone.

8

The Teenage Brain

The recent conversation I'd had in prison regarding the group's inability to express their emotions in a healthy way didn't leave me for some time. Therefore, a week or two later, I was inclined to delve into my old training notes on the teenage brain. A few months earlier, I had taken part in a webinar led by a company called Children in Scotland. Although the young men we worked with were aged between eighteen and twenty-three years old, I read that the prefrontal cortex doesn't develop fully until we are twenty-five, so I figured this research would be relevant. Especially because the prefrontal cortex is the part of the brain which is responsible for decision-making, social behaviour, judgement and impulse control – something which many of the young people I've met in prison seemed to struggle with.

My handwritten notes were just what I needed to make more sense of it all. As I read from my journal, it put me in mind of the young people I've worked with at the prison and secure units over the years.

Children in Scotland Webinar – The Teenage Brain 2021

Language is extremely important. Research in neuroscience and psychology suggests that the way emotions are described and discussed can influence how individuals understand and respond to their feelings. If emotions are repeatedly mis-labelled, a person may begin to interpret their experiences through this label, even if it doesn't truly reflect what they are actually feeling. For example, if a teen is told that they are angry all the time, then they may begin to believe this about themselves. In reality, the underlying emotion may be something different, such as stress or burnout. However, over time, the teenager may start to identify as an angry person and behaves as such, rather than dealing with the core problem.

The reward centre of the brain is particularly active during adolescence, making teenagers more sensitive to rewards than children or adults. As a result, some teens may disregard small rewards and instead, seek greater incentives. This explains why risk-taking behaviour in teens is so common. How can we encourage safer risk-taking behaviour? Perhaps from taking part in a hobby? For example, when dancing in front of an audience there may be a sense of danger due to pre-show nerves, but there's also that sense of pleasure and achievement, in the form of a round of applause and praise at the end of the show.

The reward centre of the brain changes with age, so for example, something that you found enthusing at age ten, could potentially spark zero satisfaction as a teenager. Teens often need something much bigger. This is how risk-taking behaviour comes around. Their brain craves the satisfaction that this behaviour rewards.

The more that you partake in potentially unsafe behaviour as a teenager, the more likely these habits will become wired into the brain. During the late teen years, these new brain connections start to become deeply ingrained. Because of neuroplasticity, (the brain's ability to rewire itself and grow), this can change, but it can be difficult. If you have teenage years where you take part in positive rewarding behaviours instead, transferrable life skills are more likely to be embedded.

Reading my old journal from training gave me a lot to think about it. Firstly, I had a deeper understanding of the emotional labels that we mistakenly place on young people. I realised how detrimental this could be. Knowing this made me wonder if there was more that I could do in my sessions to encourage emotional intelligence and self-awareness. Secondly, the training reminded me of the beneficial performance aspect of dance, especially aiding those who crave a high from uncertainty and risk. Holding a dance showcase would be a healthy way to give our participants this buzz. I'd made up my mind: by the end of the year, we'd host a dance showcase in the prison. We'd prepare the group to perform in front of an audience. This was my new goal.

9

Masks

Several weeks later, I began to feel a little uneasy in Gary's presence. Have you ever had your back turned from someone yet you could still somehow feel them stare straight through you? Even through you couldn't see them. That's what it felt like with Gary. I avoided eye contact as much as possible.

It was one of those days where most of our regulars were absent. So, we had Gary and two new boys. They were younger, and they acted as such. Gary was really overdoing it, trying to impress them.

As soon as Gary entered the space, he greeted me by asking, "Did you wear that lipstick for me?"

Yeah, because you're such a catch, pal. Is it the "piss off" tattoo or the orange polo shirt that gets me going? I'm spoilt for choice.

The two younger boys burst out laughing at my expense, and at that my inside jokes were interrupted. I could feel my cheeks burning. Had I been wearing too much make-up? Was it inappropriate? I liked to wear a little eyeliner and lippy, as it made me feel more confident. I also thought it made me look a little older, and therefore less close in age to some of the young men I was teaching. I had a baby face without my war paint on. Despite my sudden spout of self-doubt, I jokingly rolled my eyes and continued with the lesson. After our warm-up and team-building games, Sam and I taught a simple hip-hop dance. I cut it short, as I could tell we were losing them. They weren't fully present in the moment. I caught a few of them glancing towards the prison officer every so often, not so subtly trying to gage his reaction to the dance. They were feeling self-conscious; I could see right through them. This wasn't my first rodeo.

Gary started laughing quite a lot. Not from genuine happiness though. It was that same laugh that he used during his first week at dance, the one to mask his embarrassment. I attempted to regain their attention.

"Any questions, guys?"

"Aye. What's your phone number?" Gary asked slyly.

I inwardly cringed as I crossed my arms and shot him an unimpressed glance.

"Gary, that's enough," Sam snapped, "questions about the dance." She had been working with me for long enough to know that comebacks were not my strong suit. Well, at least not ones that I could say aloud.

Next, we attempted to teach the boys a duet. Notice how I use the word "attempt" – Gary point-blank refused. The duet consisted of lots of contact work, mainly lifts, and a variety of weight-sharing balances.

Gary poorly attempted to rationalise his decision. "Am no' doin' that. Guys don't dance like that wae each other. That's for poofs. I'll do it with you or Sam but no' with another lad. Wit a riddy."

I immediately thought back to Glennon Doyle's words from her memoir, my all-time favourite book, *Untamed*: "Boys who believe that open, vulnerable connection between men is shameful will violently hate gay boys."

The following week, we made some progress with Gary. At the start of class, we played a creative game which he excelled at. I was stunned. In our game, we had the group form a circle and we placed a chair in the middle. One at a time, the participants entered the circle and had to create a shape or an action using the chair. They had to imagine that the chair wasn't a chair. It could be anything they wanted. The aim was to think outside the box. I expected Gary to be too proud to take part, as it was brand-new and out of everyone's comfort zone. My assumption was wrong. Gary used the chair as a surfboard, a hat, weights, and much more.

Later, we gave the duets from the previous session another attempt. Gary abandoned it within five minutes. I was disappointed, as I thought we were making some progress. However, I knew this wasn't a coincidence. The two younger participants were still attending the session. Brandy and Kieran were not there to lead the pack with positivity. Gary was the leader today, and he was using his powers for evil! (OK, so I know I'm being a little dramatic here, but you know what I'm saying.) What if Gary only appeared as the leader? I think he was behaving in this way because he was adapting his energy based on the other personalities in the room. He could sense that Sam and I hadn't won over the two new boys yet. He could sense that they didn't see value in the dance class. So, he conformed, like a chameleon. In this situation, I don't see someone who's being a nuisance. I see someone who's in survival mode, and I feel for them. I wasn't always this way. I often look back to the class-clown types at my high school and how I felt about them at the time. Their behaviour and teasing would annoy me so much. I now look back and see them through a different lens.

Later in the day, Gary interrupted my teaching through asking, "What's even the point of being here? Why are we doing this?" He had such a defiant tone while speaking, as if he was itching for an argument. Fortunately, I didn't give him one. The young men in there were used to power play. Gary was trying to push my buttons to see how I'd react. He wanted to know if I was a pushover or if I was the dance-teacher version of Cruella de Vil. To his confusion, my response did not fit in either box.

"You want to know why you come to the dance class? There are so many reasons!" I replied in a chirpy yet solid manner. "Firstly, you should know that dance is great for our brain health! I recently read a book called *Spark* by John Ratey. In the book, the author talks about how cardio exercise, such as dance, can send blood to the part of the brain that's used for learning and memory. This means if you've got to study for an exam, the best time to do this is after your dance class."

Gary stared at me blankly, so I continued at a very quick pace.

"Not to mention the benefits for our physical health. I bet when you guys go to the gym, you only lift weights. You neglect the cardio. Am I right?"

I knew to ask this because of how out of breath they all would get after a simple warm-up. I got a few nods.

"Well, you know yourself that here at dance class, we work on strength training and cardio! Best of both worlds. You know that cardio training is good for your heart and lungs, so this can help prevent things like heart and lung disease. I know you're a bit young to be thinking of that now, but prevention is better than cure. Can I get an amen?"

I stopped briefly to allow appreciation of my quick wit. No one laughed. *Ugh, my humour is wasted on you people*, I thought.

"Oh wait, I almost forgot the best part," I squeaked with enthusiasm, "the cardio exercise we do in the dance class releases happy hormones in the body, such as endorphins. So, coming down to dance is good for your mental health too."

I was met with silence (for once).

"Does that answer your question, Gary?" I asked coyly.

"Ehh yeah, suppose," he answered. He seemed a little dazed, though I could see him quickly fixing his face, an attempt to come across as nonchalant. The poor bugger was probably wishing he never asked – I gave him an earful!

A few weeks later, I left Sam to fend for herself – I took annual leave to go on a beach holiday with my former situationship... Yep, that's right, red-flag man and I finally became official... but that's a story for another time. The following week, I returned with my new sun-kissed skin. My freckles were out and my cheeks were bronzed, so I decided not to put foundation on for once. I didn't even paint my go-to black wings at the corners of my eyes. I had just got a lash lift for the holiday, so I figured that was good enough. Or so I thought. My light-brown hair sat just passed my shoulders; my golden highlights were more prominent due to the sun. I wore black leggings with a navy-blue hoodie alongside my white Nike trainers.

The group swaggered in, and Gary was the first to approach me.

"This is the first time I've seen you without make-up on. Could you not be arsed this morning?"

I was mortified. I didn't have a witty comeback, not even an internal one for my personal entertainment. Nada. I patched him and greeted the rest of the boys. I couldn't help but feel offended. Who was he, or any man for that matter, to comment on how a woman looks without invitation? First, he gave me unwanted advances because I had make-up on and then he tried to humiliate me for choosing the *au naturel* look. I could never win! I was frustrated with myself for not using this moment as a teaching opportunity. I know you may be thinking that I'm taking it to heart and that what he said wasn't so bad. But it wasn't just what he said; it was the way he said it; it was the way he looked at me.

The following week, I had forgotten all about Gary's comment. I was too proud of him to be annoyed. He had finally learnt the contact duet he'd been avoiding for weeks. He even performed it with Brandy as his partner. I saw the real Gary that day. He finally took his mask off, just for a little while. He didn't make any of his usual smart-arse comments. He just put his head down and got on with it. There was a buzz in the room. The two younger boys weren't there; they packed it in a week ago. So maybe Gary felt safer to be himself. Brandy and Kieran were a positive influence (well, at least in the dance classes they were). They almost always seemed joyful, curious, and amused. Evolving neuroscience shows that emotions can spread. It's called emotional contagion. This means that if we are interacting with someone who is experiencing a certain emotion, it can be natural for us to subconsciously feel that emotion too. This can be a blessing or a curse, depending on the circumstance and depending on the emotion.

I don't need an article to teach me about emotional contagion after my experience with Brandy and Kieran. I'd be in a room with them for two minutes and a bad day would be erased. I'd be smiling and laughing alongside them in no time. I could see this happening with Gary. I guess it's like herd mentality. I used to always say, "Be a sheepdog, not a sheep." In other words, don't be a follower; try to lead and be your own person. But after recent reflection, I've realised that this is easier said than done. How can we expect young people to be their own person when they're not sure of who they are? Or worse, when they know who they are but are too scared to be authentic. In prisons (and even in schools), most young people are in constant survival mode. They are trying to fit in rather than gain a true sense of belonging. Brené Brown articulates this perfectly in her work. In *The Gifts of Imperfection*, she writes: "Fitting in is about assessing a situation and becoming who you need to be to be accepted. Belonging, on the other hand, doesn't require us to change who we are; it requires us to be who we are."

We live in a world which revolves around fitting in. Even as grown adults, we constantly follow what's trending, from the food we eat and the clothes we wear to the hashtags we use. This seems harmless. But it becomes dangerous when we allow this pattern to constantly leak into our beliefs, our values and how we see the world. This is especially alarming when it happens to easily swayed, vulnerable young people. In high-school PE, boys are offered rugby while girls are offered dance. In families, it's often assumed that the woman should stay at home to look after the children while the man goes off to work. Little girls are dressed in pink while boys are dressed in blue. Boys are handed action figures while girls are given Barbies. In the workforce, we still use gendered terms such as "postman" or "fireman". Men are often perceived as having more strength and being tougher than women. People think that men don't cry, but it's perfectly acceptable for women to shed a tear. How is this fair? If we could just lead our young people away from gender stereotypes, then maybe the young men of our society wouldn't feel the need to turn to violence as a symbol for their value and acceptance in the world. They wouldn't be afraid of appearing as weak because they would view the world from a lens of equality and freedom. They wouldn't be trying so hard to fit into an unattainable box. Instead, they'd feel a sense of belonging; if to no one else, they'd belong to themselves.

10

Granny & Grandpa

A sense of belonging was not something that I was wholeheartedly feeling in my relationship at the time. Yes, red-flag man and I had become an "official" couple, but while we had our good times, just as quickly something started to feel off. I still wasn't ready to admit it to myself, and so when the weekend rolled around, I paid a visit to the folks in my life who always made me feel that I belonged – Granny and Grandpa.

Granny and Grandpa were what you'd picture as typical grandparents – my granny baked cakes and made a big deal of me visiting, while my grandpa cracked jokes and spoiled me with presents from his most recent car boot sale adventures. Grandpa loved a car boot sale. When I was little, my sister and I would have sleepovers at their house, and Grandpa would wake us up early to go to the boot sale, teaching us how to haggle and find bargains. I hadn't gone to a boot sale in years, mostly because I was too old for a sleepover – but that didn't stop me from reaping the benefits. Almost any time I'd visit, there would be a small collection of gifts that Grandpa had bought for me, either from the boot sale or the charity shop. This was his way of being thoughtful and showing love. It would always be something that he picked out specially with excitement, as he'd be sure I'd love it. Sometimes the gifts would be fantastic, but other times... let's just say Gramps missed the mark. When he found out I watched *Strictly Come Dancing*, next thing I knew, I had a collection of *Strictly* merch, including a *Strictly* water bottle, bowl and coaster... It's the thought that counts!

As I walked into their cosy bungalow, Granny was sitting on her beige armchair – headphones on, cup of coffee in hand, intently watching the most recent episode of *EastEnders*. She didn't even hear me walk in. Grandpa was nowhere to be found, but his belongings were cluttered everywhere. At least twenty clocks surrounded the room – Grandpa was a big clock collector; it was his thing. Any time I needed a watch fixed or the battery changed, he was my guy. He was my guy for most things actually; if something needed fixing, he'd be able to work his magic.

"Oh, hen! You startled me; I didn't even see you walk in. Can I get you a cup of tea?"

"No, no, Granny, let me get it! How are you?" I softly replied, grateful for the distraction from my disastrous dating life.

As I put the kettle on, Granny retold the plot from a movie she'd watched recently. She then updated me on how the rest of our family were keeping – Granny's siblings and their children. The conversation was interrupted by my grandpa strolling in, Lidl shopping bags in hand, with a cheesy grin. He was happy to see me, but this didn't stop him singing away to himself, head-bopping and taking his shopping bags to the kitchen, before he even said hello.

"Grandpa, that song you're singing… is it 'I Love It' by Icona Pop?"

"Ehm, I'm not sure, hen. I think so," Gramps replied, unaware of how amused and simultaneously surprised I was. I had no idea how he would know a pop song from this century. A bit of Elvis was usually more his speed.

"Where on earth did you hear that?"

"The radio, hen."

Grandpa usually only listened to Smooth Radio or Absolute 80s. Maybe he fancied a change. My thoughts were interrupted by the time Grandpa had put his shopping away. Granny was still rolling her eyes at his silliness and I was still laughing. He sat on the sofa, next to me and opposite from Granny in her armchair.

"Hen, I have something to show you." He opened his laptop eagerly. "It's a song I found that I thought you could use in your dance classes!"

My heart melted at his sweetness. Before I knew it, Grandpa had a YouTube video on the screen, and "Born to Be Alive" by Patrick Hernandez played. I had never heard it before, but I instantly liked it. Although it sounded a tad old-fashioned, I enjoyed the optimism that radiated through me as I listened to the cheesy, upbeat music and lyrics. It was the type of song I could imagine would be played at the end of an '80s romantic-comedy film.

"Right, that's enough; she doesn't want to hear that!" Granny interrupted. "She hasn't even told us about her week yet. How's that boyfriend of yours, hen?"

While Granny and Grandpa bickered, I was glad that the boyfriend question got lost in the shuffle. I promptly changed the subject and told them about work in the prison. Although Mum and Dad didn't want to hear my stories, at least Granny and Grandpa did. Not only that, but they'd also offer pretty good advice. I started off chatting about the light-hearted, funny moments from the last few weeks. By the time I moved on to a more serious topic, Grandpa had left the room to work on his most recent fix-up project from the boot sale. I was grateful for this, as it was a sensitive topic and I wasn't sure how Grandpa would take it.

"Granny, I need your advice… My work want me and Sam to work with the protected prisoners again and I'm not sure how I feel about it."

"Remind me, what's protected prisoners?"

"Oh, sorry. So, it's prisoners who are not in the mainstream halls. They are protected from the mainstream population for various reasons. For example, let's say someone has an enemy in the mainstream population, they might be in protection for their safety. Or let's say someone is gay, they might be in protection if they've been the target of hate crimes – again, for their own safety. Those examples are the best-case scenario of the type of people you'll find in protection."

"It's coming back to me now, hen… Is the worst-case scenario you working with sex offenders?"

"Yeah," I gently replied.

"Haven't you worked with them years ago when you first started? You've done it before, haven't you?" Granny queried softly, leaning over to place her hand on mine. She could sense my worry.

"Yes, I have, but back then I didn't think much of it. I just thought, my work are asking me to do it, so I'll do it. I went in as if it was any other class standing in front of me, pretending that I wasn't in front of protected prisoners. The thing is, it worked – it was so strange. Sometimes I'd be in the middle of teaching a class and I would be in dance-teacher mode. Autopilot. Completely forgetting the danger of who was standing in front of me."

"So, what's changed?"

"Well… we were given a list of names for the protected class register. I googled some of them and found out what they've been charged with. I didn't like what I found. Honestly, I feel sick thinking about it. I haven't met them yet, but I'm going to have to stand in front of them as cheery, professional Aimee, pretending I don't know what they've done."

It wasn't just that. I'd grown up since the last time. Since then, I'd seen more instances of sexual assault on the news, in films and documentaries. I couldn't stomach it. As a woman, I could not imagine a more debilitating, horrendous crime. I also felt guilty. I'd be having a laugh with these people, allowing them to enjoy a fun dance class. Did they deserve as much? I wasn't so sure.

As if reading my mind, Granny interrupted my manic thought process. "Hen, it's not your place to judge them. They've already been judged by the court. They're in prison serving their sentence. It's not your job to analyse every single person who comes into your class. I'm not saying their crimes are forgivable – but what I am saying is that on Google, you are reading one version of the story. Try not to read any more though. There might still be people in your class who are only in protection because of the risk of hate crimes, or enemies, like you said. Well, focus on that. Don't punish yourself with feelings of guilt or worry."

It still didn't sit right with me, but I knew that my wise granny had made some good points. I was prepared to stop googling them – but I'd also be extra vigilant, keeping my wits about me in the sessions. My mind was much more at ease, and I was ready to meet the new cohort come Tuesday.

11

The Protected Prisoners

The first class with the protected prisoners went well. Oddly, I managed to block out my personal feelings towards some of them just fine. There's a weird thing that happens to me when I stand in front of a class to teach... I'm no longer Aimee; I'm now Teacher Aimee. A more confident, brave, social, and less-awkward version of myself. It's like an alter ego.

Several weeks passed and I began to feel more and more comfortable with the new group. I take pride in being a professional, so I stopped the googling and blocked the judgement out. Right up until I was left feeling unsafe – something I thought would never happen to me in the prison, what with all the security and protocols.

It was a typical Tuesday morning. I was in the performing-arts space by 8am, and I had walked there from reception alone. Sam would usually arrive closer to 8.45am, right before the class would start, due to childcare timings. I didn't need an officer to escort me, as a few years prior I had been on a prison training session which allowed me to walk around the prison by myself.

No officer had arrived yet, but I was happy with that. It gave me a chance to look over my notes with no interruptions, preparing the lessons for the day. My planning came to a halt when a female officer who I'd never met walked in with a boy from the new protected prisoners' class. His name was Gavin, and I didn't know much about him. He wasn't very outgoing or confident, but I usually managed to get quite a bit of small talk out of him. In the past few weeks, he'd told me all about his career and home life; he seemed like a normal guy. Despite this, he didn't fool me. I got a slightly weird feeling about him, but I didn't know why. It was just a feeling. Still, he was one of the few that I hadn't googled and I wanted to keep it that way, for my own sake.

"Hiya. Is it alright if I leave him here with you while I go and collect the others?" she asked casually, clearly unaware of how uncomfortable she'd just made me feel. Never in my three years of working at the prison had this ever happened.

Hell no! You realise you're trying to leave me alone with a potential rapist? Think, Aimee, think! How can you say no without making Gavin realise you don't want to be alone with him?

"Emm, I don't know if I'm allowed?" I said as a question rather than a statement, trying to make it appear as though it wasn't my personal feelings towards Gavin but me trying to do the right thing professionally. In other words, I decided to play dumb. Thankfully, it worked.

"Right, OK... we'll go and get the rest of them then," she replied with a little confusion in her tone.

Well done for your quick thinking, girl! I quietly thought to myself as they walked away.

The session went well, as usual. After lunch, we had the mainstream group, and we celebrated Brandy's birthday. We brought him in some cake from the supermarket and made everyone sing "Happy Birthday". It was sweet.

"This is my second birthday cake this week." Brandy had a mouthful of cake at this point.

"Wait, what? No way! Who else has brought you in cake?" I wondered aloud, probably a little too sceptically.

Gary chimed in next. "Nae cunts brought him in cake. It's jail cake he's on about."

"I've lost count of the amount of jail cake I've made for people in here," Kieran claimed proudly.

"What on earth is jail cake?"

For the next few minutes, the boys answered my question in depth, describing how they'd use digestive biscuits and melted chocolate to make the perfect no-bake jail cake. It was a birthday tradition in the prison, apparently. They went on in detail – any excuse for them to have a longer tea break.

The conversation progressed to what meals the birthday boy had been learning to make at his life-skills classes.

"The ladies will be in for a treat when I get out. It'll be one lucky lady, that's for sure. Ladies… get your offers in."

Sam and I laughed in response.

"That didn't sound like a no… but a suppose we've got to keep things professional in that." Brandy paused as if he was contemplating a serious matter. "Yeah, sorry. It would be a conflict of interest, wouldn't it." His tone suggested he was sad to disappoint us.

"Sorry, Brandon, you're a bit young for us anyway." I edged towards the iPod and speaker, gently hinting at halting the conversation.

"Well, what I lack in age I make up for in muscle!" Brandy flexed and kissed his biceps while the other boys cackled.

"Right, birthday boy, are you ready to lead the warm-up?"

"Aye, a wis born ready."

Over the last few weeks, Brandy had been the most consistent with attendance. This meant that we could put him through a dance leadership qualification, if he was keen. We spoke about this with him the week before and he seemed interested, so we used this session as a little trial to see if dance leadership would be his cup of tea. To help him test the waters, we tasked him with planning and delivering this week's warm up.

"How are you feeling, everyone? On a scale from one to ten?" Brandy posed the check in question with more formality than usual. We didn't even ask him to include the check-in. Soon after, Brandy blasted music from our iPod Nano through the speaker. His song choice was "Bits and Pieces" by GBX. We followed his lead, mirroring his star jumps, squats, high knees and stretches. Every so often, he briefly paused, checking his notepad to try and remember what he had planned. He was a real taskmaster – we ended up holding the plank for quite a lengthy time.

"Get your ass down!" he motioned to Kieran, who looked as though he was trying the downward dog yoga pose rather than our usual plank. "You should know the drill by now, boys!"

Next, we moved into holding a side plank, with one elbow and forearm on the ground and one arm stretched to the sky, one hip facing the floor, with the sides of our feet balanced on the ground.

"Come here often?" Brandy and I were accidentally facing one another. He used the opportunity to stroke his chin with his free hand while pretending to chat me up.

"Stop making me laugh or I'm going to fall!"

We continued the warm-up, and when we were done, Brandy thanked us for taking part.

"Well done, lads and lassies. Excellent work. Thank you for your participation. We've got those endorphins going now, don't we!"

"He's spending too much time with you, Aimee. He even sounds like you now with all that endorphin talk!" Sam teased.

We got on with the remainder of the class, and before finishing up for the day, we privately gave Brandy some leadership feedback. We praised his high energy demonstrations, clear communication and motivation techniques. However, we asked him to try it next time without stopping to look at his notes, although, we did praise him for being prepared and devising a plan. He seemed eager to try again next week.

Even though I put a brave face on in the mainstream class, I still couldn't shake the situation from that morning with Gavin and the prison officer. The more I thought about it, I realised I was mad. Mad that I'd been put in such an awkward, uncomfortable and potentially dangerous position. When I got home, I caved. That's right, I googled Gavin. I had his full name from the register, so I typed away, also adding the town he told me he was from; surely that would help narrow down the results. Bingo: an article popped up with vivid details of his crime. I felt sick. The report described a violent and disturbing attack on a stranger. My jaw fell open as I read on. It spoke of his attempt to sexually assault and murder the stranger, who happened to be a young woman. Thankfully, he was caught before his violence could escalate. Thought after thought swirled in my brain, causing a pounding headache. *Thank God that scumbag was arrested. What the hell am I doing, teaching predators like that? Wait a minute… I was almost left alone with him. Alone. What on earth was that prison officer thinking? What would have happened if I was alone with him? I suppose, hypothetically, I was considered "safe enough" this morning. I did have a safety alarm that I could push at any time in case of emergency.*

As I skimmed through the article again, I stopped gaslighting myself. This guy was fucked up. His victim was a random woman. This was a targeted attack against a random woman. *So, he hates all women? Wait – I'm a woman. So, I do not feel safe in his presence. Not only that, but I also no longer feel safe with him knowing my name or anything about me. What if, when he gets out, he types my name and the company I work for into Google. He'd easily be able to find me. What if he now has a vendetta against me specifically because he could sense I was uncomfortable being in a room alone with him? What if he's easily able to find me and he now also hates me? What then?*

12

Trust No One

The following week, my thought process regarding Gavin, and people like him, had changed slightly. I stopped worrying about my safety. The worry hadn't vanished; it simply shifted. My concerns were now fuelled with moral dilemmas. As I drove to the prison that morning, I thought of the victims. My heart sank for them. My blood boiled for them. Was I a bad person for teaching their attackers? I used to think that's what made me a good person – the point was rehabilitation. But, when I actually thought about it, I couldn't fathom how a once-a-week dance class had some magical powers to rehabilitate a sex offender. Whereas rehabilitation for our mainstream group? I had seen it first-hand, and in the cases where I was yet to see it unfold, I still had strong faith in it. The point of the prison project was to reduce the risk of antisocial and criminal behaviour. I wholeheartedly believed that the project had the power to make this positive change, especially in the young men who had committed petty crimes. Over the years, I saw prisoners working as a team, building positive friendships and learning how to communicate more effectively. I saw young men gaining leadership qualifications while developing self-belief and inspiration for a better life after prison. I saw prisoners get clean from alcohol and drugs so that they could attend the dance sessions. I saw them replace their vices in the form of a natural high – a sense of purpose, endorphins and laughter. It sounds cheesy, but it's true. I really did see the mental health improve in the prisoners I taught.

Speaking of the mainstream prisoners, fortunately, that was the group I taught first that morning. I was relieved at the opportunity to ease myself into my teacher alter ego before it was time to see Gavin again. We began the lesson with Brandy's second go of leading the warm-up. He did a brilliant job, taking on the feedback that Sam and I gave him in the previous session. "Shots" by LMFAO played as Brandy called out what seemed to be his tagline: "Shake what ya mamma gave ya." Meanwhile, all us participants were shaking our shoulders up and down to the beat of the music. Star jumps, box steps and box slides followed, without Brandy having to look down at his notepad once.

"This leadership stuff suits me, so it does," Brandy announced as the music stopped.

The rest of the class consisted of practising dances for our small, upcoming showcase, with our usual tea break in between. During the tea break, I overheard the boys slagging off the protected prisoners, referring to them as "beasts". I let them. So did Sam; she had been feeling as conflicted as I had over the past few weeks. I didn't join in or acknowledge what they were saying, but I didn't stop it either. I know that doesn't sound very professional, but if I chose to tell the boys off, that would be like sticking up for sex offenders, and that was something I just wasn't prepared to do.

"The annual panto's fast approaching. Can you teach us some moves for it?" Kieran asked as he served diluting juice to the others.

"You're the poster boy of youth theatre," Brandy teased, saying *poster boy* with a hint of sarcasm. "Why don't you teach us the moves, Mr Poster Boy?"

"What kind of moves? What part do you play?" I asked.

"Can't tell you that; it's gotta be a surprise!"

"You've got to tell us something so we know what to choreograph. What vibe are you going for?"

"Hmm… something jolly, I reckon!"

"Naw, not something jolly," Gary interrupted with his usual smirk. "That guy's got no shame."

How they roped Gary into performing in the panto, I'll never know.

"Ma da's coming to watch the show. It's the first time he's gonna see me since I've been in here, and that's quite a few years. I'm never gonna live this down, am I?" Brandy commented while pacing. Nothing was ever that serious with him. At least that's what he wanted us to think. The rest of the tea break consisted of him sharing some questionable stories of his drunken antics as a kid.

After lunch, it was time to work with the protected prisoners again. It was time to see Gavin again.

He didn't come to the session. Phew – I had at least another week to process the unprofessional disgust I felt towards him. I didn't know why he didn't come down. I didn't care. I didn't even ask about it.

As I started teaching alongside Sam, I instantly felt better. Autopilot, alter ego Aimee was back at it again! The thought of being in a room with those people was worse than actually being in the room. Although I knew better, I managed to relax into things and kind of enjoy it – just how I would have if I had been teaching any other group. This felt no different. When I was younger, I used to believe that if I was ever unlucky enough to be around a "bad guy", I would get a gut feeling. I used to believe that if I was ever around an absolute psycho, or even a somewhat dangerous person, I would just know it. I thought that I would feel it in my bones – that my skin would crawl and my heart would race, and I'd become more alert due to a sinking feeling in my stomach. I have now learnt that we cannot rely on instinct. Sometimes, even if you know better, these instinctual feelings do not come.

I realised all of this when I got home that evening, after my most recent Google spree. There was a boy in the protected prisoners' session who'd been attending for a few weeks. He was extremely quiet. I never got a bad feeling about him, like I had previously with Gavin, but I also found him tricky to read. Secretly hoping that he was in protection only for his own safety, such as having an enemy in mainstream, I typed his name into the search engine. Just like that, an article with his photo appeared. As I read about his crimes, my stomach churned. Long story short, he created a false online identity and arranged a meeting with a young girl. The encounter turned into a violent and terrifying sexual assault. The article was much more disturbing and graphic, but I'll spare you the details.

I'd had enough. It was all getting a bit too much for me. I felt overwhelmed, disgusted, and riddled with guilt for allowing people like that into my class. I knew it wasn't my choice, but still, I couldn't help but feel guilty. Out of all the emotions, guilt was probably the one I struggled with the most.

Grandpa's voice played in my head repeatedly as I read the article: "Trust no one," is what he always said. It never rang truer for me until this moment. Growing up, he'd always warned us to protect ourselves when out and about. Before going on holiday, he'd remind us girls to "stick together" and advise us not to wear our best jewellery in case someone was to snatch it from our necks. As bubbly and happy as Grandpa appeared, it was like he saw the worst in people. I always just thought he was overprotective and cautious because he loved us so much. That was probably true, but now, for the first time, I realised there was more to it than that. As someone who naturally sees the good in everyone, even when they haven't earned my trust yet, this was hard for me to come to terms with.

13

One-a-Day

As usual, I walked straight into Granny and Grandpa's small bungalow without knocking. I had called them ten minutes beforehand to ask if I could visit, and of course they were delighted to see me. Grandpa had set out a Müller Corner yoghurt for me and Granny had made me tea. It was sat on the coffee table at my usual seat – opposite Granny's armchair and next to Grandpa.

"Hi, hen. Your one-a-day's there for you on the table," Grandpa called from the kitchen as I entered the living room. "One-a-day" is what Grandpa referred to the Müller yoghurts that he would buy for me and my sister when we stayed over as kids, during the summer holidays. I didn't really know why he called them that, maybe because he knew that we liked them, so he always tried to get us to have one at least once a day, although he always reminded us we could have more than one if we wanted. It was endearing.

The reminder of our childhood one-a-day treat got me thinking. What were the one-a-days in my life? What were my non-negotiables? What did I enjoy so much that I had to do it at least once a day? I imagine for most people, their one-a-days would come from necessity rather than from intentional self-care, such as tooth-brushing or making the bed in the morning. What if we all dedicated our one-a-days to things that are good for our well-being – maybe gratitude practice, getting more sleep, meditation or exercise? Imagine if we could make these small acts as habitual as our autopilot one-a-days. I wonder what difference that would make in the prisoners I've met. It would take some discipline, but I reckon it would be worth it…

Grandpa made his way back to the living room as I quietly finished my yoghurt. He wore his usual checkered shirt with braces to hold his trousers up. He was very tall and broad, so much so that I often forgot how old he was. When his smoker's cough made an appearance, I was instantly reminded. Before diving straight in with all my worries, I tried to kickstart conversation in a more light-hearted way, retelling Brandy's stories of his wild, drunken antics. I thought this would be best while Grandpa was still in the room. I wasn't sure if Granny had mentioned that I'd been working with protected prisoners.

"Drink is no good. It's bad news – makes people act in all sorts of stupid ways." He said it with a worried tone, as if I was the one involved in the drunken antics rather than Brandy. I didn't take it personally – Grandpa was a recovered alcoholic, so he knew all about how drinking could change people. He never actually told me this; it was my mum. She told me how growing up could be extremely tough at times for her, Granny, and her siblings, all because of Grandpa's drinking problem. She didn't give away much else, keeping a lot close to her chest. Despite this, she still had so much love for my grandpa, and they always seemed to get along well. Mum told me that Grandpa managed to quit drinking for good when my sister and I were very little. That explains why I have no memories of Grandpa other than the warm, caring, thoughtful man who sat beside me.

"Yeah, I know, Grandpa. Don't worry, I don't get into trouble like that or drink too much."

"That's what I like to hear."

Around ten minutes later, Grandpa went for a nap, giving me and Granny some alone time. I spilled my guts out. There was something about my granny – I could say anything and everything without a second thought. She is the least judgemental person I have ever met. She always has time and patience for me. I told her everything I had been worrying about over the last few weeks, and my new findings from my latest Google spree.

After empathising with my concern and shock, she ended our conversation with this: "Aimee, these people are going to end up back in our society one day, whether we like it or not. You can't possibly know if the dance project can make a dent in their rehabilitation and you can't control that, but you can play a small part in leaving them better off than how you found them. At least you know you will have tried to help someone re-enter our society as a better version of themselves. That's got to count for something."

14

Breaking Point

In the weeks that followed, Sam and I confided in one another about our personal feelings towards working with some of the protected prisoners. She seemed more upset than me; she'd even organised a Zoom meeting with our boss to discuss the matter. She asked if she could mention me in the meeting, to explain that I felt the same way and it wasn't just a Sam problem. Without hesitation, I agreed. Albeit nervous, I was glad to get this off my chest. I was warned that they would bring me into the call after some one-to-one time with Sam.

I spent the days beforehand overthinking what I would say and how I would say it. Although prison talk was usually off limits with my parents, I had spoken with them about what was going on. I knew they would try to help me figure this out. When I was brought into the call, it was clear that the conversation was already well under way. Sam was crying. This was out of character for Sam; she was one tough cookie, and it took a lot to rattle her. At the time, I assumed it was because she was so worked up and upset about some of the crimes that the protected prisoners had committed. Looking back, I'm not so sure. Maybe her tears were from the frustration of the conversation not going to plan.

"Aimee, I'm sure that Sam has filled you in on why we're here today. I understand that you've also had some concerns about working with the prisoners in protection?"

This is a positive start, I thought to myself, *my boss seems open*. And with that, I candidly spilled all my concerns from the past few weeks, one being my safety.

"I've been speaking to my mum and dad about the situation. They're worried about my safety. They're worried that when these guys get released, they know my name and where I work. They're worried in case I get a stalker or that I'm in any sort of danger from a sex offender being able to find me."

I know I was a bit old to be blaming my mum and dad. It just felt like a good safety net. I also felt that I would be taken more seriously if I was bringing up the concerns of my parents, who were older and wiser than me.

My boss gave a small chuckle – perhaps trying to lighten the mood.

"I think your parents are being a bit overprotective. You'd have more chance of getting hurt by someone random on the street than from a young lad you've met briefly in prison."

OK, this is not going well, I thought to myself, *she is not taking me seriously, and even worse, she thinks I've been watching too many true crime documentaries.*

"But Sam and I have googled their crimes, and if you were to read these articles, you'd see it's not that far of a reach. Some of these guys have gone out of their way to intentionally hurt random women. I'm also just feeling guilty that we have rapists and child molesters in our class. It's just something I can't get my head around. I don't know how someone could do such a thing."

"Aimee, I hear your concerns, I really do. But in reality, some of the young people in your mainstream group may have committed equally serious crimes. If we decide to exclude participants based on offence type, we start to engage in a moral ranking of crimes – asking whether rape is worse than murder, for example – and that's a complex, and potentially problematic, road to go down."

I didn't know what to say. I wasn't prepared for this debate, and frankly it was above my paygrade. I felt a throbbing headache coming on.

"I do need to flag something else," my boss continued. "It's not appropriate to look up the young people in your sessions online. Going forward, we'll make sure that's clarified in the staff handbook." She paused, then added more gently, "I imagine it's been difficult to go to work with those details weighing on your mind. It's likely affected how you've been able to show up in the class."

Great, now she's questioning my professionalism. This is not how I thought this conversation would go at all – me leaving my fears at the side to convince my boss I wasn't letting them interfere with my job.

"No, no. I promise I have been professional and taught the class just like I would with any other group. But it's hard when you don't feel safe. Just the other week there, I was in prison by myself, before the class started, and an officer tried to leave one of the protected prisoners alone with me. I couldn't believe it. Luckily, I thought quickly on my feet and pretended I wasn't sure if I was allowed to be alone with him. I didn't want to show how uncomfortable I was because I didn't want the prisoner to realise how I felt and take it to heart. That was a really upsetting situation for me, and it's why I went home and googled the prisoner. I wanted to know what to expect if that ever happens again and I can't as easily talk my way out of it."

"Really? I'm so sorry to hear that, Aimee. That should have never happened. Do you know the officer's name so we can report it?"

"No, I don't know who she is. It was the first and only time I've ever met her. Don't worry about reporting it – I don't want to get anyone into trouble. Hopefully it was an honest mistake that doesn't happen again."

"OK, well make sure you let me know if this ever happens again, as soon as it happens."

I nodded in response, and my boss continued. "Circling back to you googling the prisoners… Knowing what they've done shouldn't influence the way you treat or interact with them in the class. Everyone should be treated the same. You work with teenagers in secure units all the time. You know that some of the kids in there are only there because they're too young to go to prison. You don't know what crimes they've committed. For all you know, it could be the same as some of the protected prisoners. You've got to think to yourself, what went horribly wrong in their lives for them to commit crimes like that? We all start life in the same way, as an innocent child. So, something has gone horrendously wrong for these young people."

"Yeah, I get that." It was all I could muster. I was beginning to feel guilty again.

Sam was quiet – she seemed to calm down since the interrogation was no longer aimed at her. I could see that her watery eyes had eased up.

"You know, you don't need to work on the prison project anymore if you don't want to. Just let me know and I'll switch you onto another project and someone else can take your place." She said this with a sense of softness that she'd earlier neglected.

I didn't respond right away. In that moment, I saw that her intentions were good all along, even if her delivery didn't always land well. She strongly believed in the power of rehabilitation.

I took a few seconds to think. I didn't know what I was expecting from this meeting, but this wasn't it. Did I want to take her up on her offer to leave? No, I realised that I did not. I didn't think the conversation would turn in this way. I was naively hoping that our boss would instead let us have some say on which prisoners attended our dance class. I say naively because, of course, funding has a big part to play. If we were to pick and choose who could attend our sessions, numbers of attendees would decrease, and this looks bad on paper, especially to our funders. Although my boss advocated about inclusivity, and yes, I'm sure she really felt that way, I wasn't blind to the financial pressures behind the direction of this conversation. Despite this, I decided to stay on the prison project, and that meant I had to swallow my feelings. Sam stayed too. We were both passionate about all the good we had achieved with Brandy, Kieran, and even Gary. Those boys had made mistakes which resulted in their incarceration, yes, but they weren't bad people; they had just done some bad things... Haven't we all?

15

Throwback

It was a typical training day, working from home. I'd received the Zoom link; this was the new norm after the pandemic. I waited patiently for the host to start the meeting as I made myself a cuppa. Although I missed in-person socialising, I was thankful that the training was via Zoom. I'd just returned from a lunch break 5k run and I did not look put together. I was hoping I could erase my blemishes with a natural-looking filter. I messed around with my camera settings, and voilà: my rosy cheeks and lack of make-up were not a problem.

The host began the meeting, and I began taking notes right away. I learn best through writing everything down. It was an all-day training course based on facilitation of the arts in prisons. As much as I looked forward to the learning around the topic itself, the thought of sitting at a laptop all day wasn't so appealing.

Flash forward to three hours later and, to my surprise, I could have sat there and listened for three hours more.

I felt so inspired. Our trainer, Janice, was so passionate and full of life. She had the perfect balance of stats and research, alongside opening the floor to discussions and pertinent storytelling. Her eyes lit up when she talked, and despite talking with us through a screen, she managed to present in such an animated way. Her drive was contagious; I could tell she cared deeply about her work. She made me feel like a superhero. I know that sounds cringe, but she really went deep into why we do what we do. It's not just for the sake of teaching the arts; the benefits lie so much deeper.

Janice covered so much, from ACEs, to rehabilitation, to tips for engagement. She also discussed how she delivered her specialist art form within the prison. Janice was a drama teacher. I remembered going to see a few of her productions years ago, as several boys who attended dance were featured. To be honest, when I first heard that drama was being taught in prisons, my brain immediately went straight to the idea of reading scripts and refining performance techniques. I had no idea. After watching the productions, I realised this was not the case at all. I had just assumed what drama class would be like, and I now realise that many are likely to assume when it comes to the art form that I teach. Most non-dancers don't realise how much creativity, empowerment, and leadership skills are involved in our dance sessions, amongst many other advantages. I can't believe I made this mistake with drama; I should have known better.

When watching the prison drama productions, I could tell that the boys had collaborated in writing the script. Meaningful and personal topics were explored, such as, what does it mean to be a man in the twenty-first century? In some of the productions, the actors had written letters to their younger selves or to their family members and read them aloud for the audience to hear. They were learning to be brave and vulnerable, in addition to challenging perceptions on the chosen theme. It wasn't all heavy though; there were some very funny and interactive moments with the audience. Everyone was laughing and having a good time. The boys were able to express many sides of their personalities, even their cheeky and playful sides. This work was important. Watching these drama shows is what inspired me to delve into more hard-hitting topics in the prison dance class. So, during the Zoom training with the brains behind the process, I felt a little star-struck.

The training day gave me a lot to consider. That same evening, I felt empowered when talking to my family about it. Understandably, my parents still didn't like the idea of me working in the prison, even more so now after the protected prisoners' fiasco. I, on the other hand, felt much better about the situation. A few months had passed since the awkward conversation with my boss, and since then, almost all the protected prisoners from the previous group had fizzled out. Some had been released, some had moved to a new prison, and some just had no interest in attending anymore. This was the fresh start that Sam and I needed. Before we knew it, we had a small, new cohort of protected prisoners to work with. We decided to no longer agonise over the ethics of it all. Yes, we had our personal viewpoints on the matter, but it was out of our control, so we tried to focus on the positive. We knew that there were young men in our protected prisoner class who were not in mainstream only for their own protection, not because of any sexual- or domestic-related crimes. We tried to remind ourselves of this when our apprehension creeped up.

It wasn't as easy to crush the apprehension of my parents. To reassure them (and myself), I'd try to tell stories of the positive impact of my work. Notice how I use the word "try". Sometimes my dad didn't want to hear it. That's how much he didn't agree with this element of my job. I soon realised it wasn't just about my safety. My dad didn't believe that prisoners could change, even the boys in mainstream. I tried to prove him wrong through telling him all about my learning from the Zoom training. I had his attention, and the conversation progressed to some of my experiences on the inside. I told him about the first group of young prisoners I ever taught. I gave a short and sweet version of the story that follows.

Three years earlier...

I was twenty-one years old and had very recently graduated from full-time education. I had been on the job for only two months. Up until this point, I had lived a sheltered life. I was very naive. I was an apprentice dance teacher and so I worked alongside my brilliant colleague and friend, Katie. I was lucky because the pressure was totally lifted. I got to turn up and take part without the worry of teaching. Katie and I had a similar bond to the one which Sam and I shared. We would carpool on our way to the prison, and Katie would call it "Tinder Tuesdays". I'm sure you can imagine why: I'd update Katie on all my dating stories while receiving some sisterly advice in return. Katie taught me so much about participatory dance. She discussed the challenges and solutions; she gave me some teaching tips; and she went over her preferred teaching methodologies.

I remember my first day so clearly. I was so nervous. Luckily, it was a nice group of young boys and there were only four of them. They were all friendly enough. There was no weird behaviour or comments made (to my surprise). I found out what a few of them were in for. I would never ask; I just overheard their conversations. To my relief, it was all petty crimes, like stealing and drunken fighting. Katie led a follow-on warm-up. She taught a few of the warm-up moves slowly before getting the boys to try it with music. This was great for building their confidence. Next, we played a fitness game and learnt a street dance, which they loved. It was to the song "Turn Down for What", which was a big hit with the boys.

We had a tea break, and I noticed Katie making casual conversation with the group, trying to build a relationship. She made this look so easy. I didn't know where to begin. It's not like you could ask them the usual, like, "So what are you doing at the weekend?" Or, "Any plans tonight?" That would not be appropriate. I didn't want to put my foot in it, so I stayed silent. I was an awkward wee soul. Katie, on the other hand, seemed so relaxed. She asked things like, "What's for dinner tonight then?" I was stunned at how she could wangle a full conversation out of this topic. She'd then ask what music they liked and got everyone to write a few songs down. She promised she'd add this to the playlist for next week. I remember thinking how that was a lovely gesture. I got the sense it made them feel heard and seen, that their input was valued.

It got to the end of the session and one of the boys asked me, "So, Aimee, how've you found your first day in the prison?"

It was only in that moment I realised I had not said one word until that point. I laughed and softly replied, explaining how much fun it was.

A week or two later, we acquired a new member. His name was Logan. He was the class clown of the group, and he was always trying to chat me up (I left this part of the story out when speaking with my dad; I didn't want to give him a heart attack). I remember he would say corny chat-up lines, like, "Do you wear contacts? Oh wait, that's just a sparkle in your eye." I would be buckled with cringe and laughter, as would the other boys. It was all in good nature. He was a nineteen-year-old boy full of confidence and banter. It was to be expected. He was always cracking jokes and seemed like a happy person. His ADHD made it extremely difficult for him to focus during the sessions. We tried our best to be accommodating, allowing for breaks and trying to fit the lesson into short bursts.

Logan would express his gratitude for our inclusivity. It was clear that this was not something he was used to. I remember him telling us about his experience in primary school. He told us that the teachers couldn't handle his disruptive energy and behaviour, so he was always "papped away to the computing room alone". He explained how there weren't enough classroom assistants to support him, so he'd be given a game to play on the computer. If I was teaching a pupil who behaved in such a disruptive way that hindered his right for an education, I'd be inclined to dig a little deeper as to why this behaviour was occurring. However, I know that teachers are overworked and under strain. This is where the system is failing. I could see the result of this failed system first-hand. Logan didn't know how to tell the time;

he couldn't read a clock. Eventually, the youth work team in the prison taught him. He also struggled with written work. On any occasion where we asked the boys to fill in booklets, I would scribe for him. He'd tell me what to write, but he didn't have enough confidence in his literacy skills to work independently. He also couldn't tie his shoelaces… we can't blame the school system for that one. The more he got to know us, the more he'd open up about some of the darker points of his childhood. He was such a storyteller by nature, so he was able to dress it up in whatever way he liked, usually through comedy. I remember him telling us how, at ten years old, he saw his mum's latest boyfriend buying heroine. His house was a bit of a "party gaff" while he was growing up. Not a party for him, but for his parent. I got the sense that he was neglected for a lot of his childhood.

I explained all of this to my dad. He didn't bite. My last attempt was this: "Dad, how would you feel if you were watching a film where a small child is neglected or abused? We watch these movies, and we see the sad little child alone in their room with a hopeless expression. We feel for them. We know they deserve more. We know this wasn't their fault; they've been unlucky in life. It's not fair. Have you ever considered that the prisoner I talk about was once that same child?"

16

Substance Misuse

Talking with my dad about Logan brought up a lot of old memories. I began to wonder how some of the boys we used to teach were doing now. Had they managed to stay out of prison? Had our time with them made a positive difference? Curiosity got the better of me, so I decided to ask the poster boy of performing arts, aka Kieran, someone who's clocked up more jail time than a Monopoly board.

"How's Adam getting on?"

"Aw, he's a bit of a gimp to be honest. I never liked him, so a wouldn't know."

"Aw, OK. What about Darren?"

"Yeah, a heard he's up in shots now. He got eighteen year. Apparently, he bust up the whole hall and battered four screws."

I gave him a look as if to say: how do you even know this? He must have sensed what I was thinking, as he gave me a sly look while tapping his nose several times.

"I don't get it. Does he not just want to keep his head down and have an easy life?"

"Aye, well, in this prison he was big fish in a small pond. Folk dinnae want tae mess with him here. He wanted that same respect over there. He's a small fish in a big pond over there, so he probably wanted to make a name fae himself."

I nodded in realisation. It made complete sense. "OK, so what about Rab?" I asked, expecting a similar answer.

I met Rab a few years back. He was in for drug dealing. He was a chilled-out wee guy, a bit of a ned, but, as my dad always says, there's a wee ned inside all of us. I remember being frustrated after a few conversations with Rab about his chosen line of work. I'd ask him if he was going to make a change and stay away from it when he got out. I was basically asking if prison had given him a reality check. He would reply by saying that he'd never give up drug dealing as he'd never find a job that would earn him that amount of money. I tried to challenge this, but in the end, it felt like I was getting nowhere. I was just one person. Of course I couldn't change his mindset on my own. But I took comfort in knowing that I was planting small seeds. Unfortunately, those seeds were never given the chance to grow.

Kieran interrupted my trip down memory lane, replying to my question with a sigh. "He's deed."

I couldn't believe it. I didn't believe it. Rab was only eighteen. Kieran's tone was too matter-of-fact for it to be true. *Surely not*, I thought to myself, *he's at it; he's showing no emotion, so it can't be true.*

"What?" I replied, followed by a tiny trickle of laughter. Don't judge me, I know I sound like a sociopath; I thought he was kidding on.

Kieran then went on to tell me the full story. Rab and some others had been taking Valium. I refer to them as "others" because I wouldn't know what else to call them after hearing this story – certainly not friends, that's for sure. Rab had overdosed. Apparently, his lips were turning blue, and he was getting extremely unwell, dipping in and out of consciousness. He asked the people he was with to call an ambulance; he told them he thought he was dying. They didn't take him seriously.

I was in shock for the rest of the session. I was probably quite passive while trying to take it all in. A few weeks ago, Kieran had mentioned the reason he was in prison. Long story short, he'd gotten into a drunken fight with a stranger. The story of Rab's death made me think of this. It made me think of the huge substance misuse problem that Scottish prisons are facing. The young prisoners are likely leaving more addicted than when they came in. They previously talked openly to me about the stuff they take when alone in their gaffs as well as the inevitable comedown. Sometimes I made no comment. Other times I challenged it. When I chose to challenge it, I was often met with the following response: "Well, we've got fuck all else to do." When I was met with a response like that, I'd think to myself, *what are they saying and what are they not saying?*

What are they not saying? "Rather than sitting alone with our thoughts, our grief, or our pain, we'd rather feel numb. We'd rather avoid our anxiety."

What are they not saying? "We are not allowed to sit with our pain. We are not allowed to feel it. We are living in a world where men are taught to hide their emotions. Men are taught toxic masculinity. How can we push our feelings down? How can we escape from our demons so we can fit in with society's expectations of a man?"

What are they not saying? "We want a temporary high. It's self-soothing. This is the only way to cope."

What are they not saying? "We are impressionable young people who have not been taught to stand against the herd. We have an innate desire to fit in with others. We want to belong; we want to connect. Even if that means getting mixed up with alcohol and drugs just because everyone else is doing it."

It can be easy for us to pass judgement on those who struggle with substance misuse. It can be easy to look down at the "junkies and alkies" of the world. But that doesn't mean that we should.

When talking about Rab's death, Kieran was so OK. He was too OK. It was as if he was telling a story about a stranger from the news. Was this a common occurrence in his world? So it didn't faze him anymore? A few weeks prior, during our dance class, one of the boys had revealed his mum had just passed away. He was only twenty-one. I can't imagine losing a parent at such an early age. To be honest, I can't imagine the pain of losing a parent at any age. But he was eerily OK. It made me wonder, are these young men hiding their true feelings as a survival instinct? Or are they experiencing dissociation due to trauma? According to an informal survey taken out by the prison's youth work team, 75% of the young people in their custody had experienced a traumatic bereavement. If that's not enough reason to take the edge off with alcohol or drugs, I'm not sure what is.

The first time I met Brandy, he was under the influence; the full reason that Kieran was in prison was due to alcohol; and now Rab was dead. Change is vital.

17

Mind Over Matter

The following week, our day at the prison was cancelled due to conflicting events and workshops lead by the youth work team. This meant I had a day to catch up with my admin, so I chose to work at our company's office. Since we were in post-Covid times, new hybrid ways of working had become the norm, so hardly anyone was in the office with me all morning. At lunchtime, I made the most of my lunch break by running a 5k at Glasgow Green. By the time I returned, I had the full office to myself – everyone else was working from home or out teaching classes.

As I worked my way through the remainder of my to-do list, I'd remembered that a few days ago, I had planned to visit Granny and Grandpa after work. I thought I better double-check it was still OK for me to come, so I called Granny's mobile number. She answered after one ring. Her voice was shaky and flustered.

"Hi, Granny. Just double checking it's OK for me to come round tonight at around—"

"Hen, you can't come round tonight. Grandpa's had an accident. I need to get hold of your mum. He's at the hospital. They say he's only got a few days left to live."

"Wait, what? What's happened?"

"Hen, I need to get hold of your mum. I've been trying non-stop and no answer. I need a lift to the hospital."

I imagine the shock and panic was why she didn't answer my question.

"I'm on my way. I'll be there in twenty minutes. Keep calling Mum."

I ended the call without any answers to my burning questions. The how or why didn't matter at that moment in time. All that mattered was getting to my granny and grandpa as fast as possible. I felt my pulse race and breathing quicken as I swiftly stumbled around the office trying to gather my things at lightning speed. My vision was blurred from streaming tears, so that didn't help. All I felt was panic and urgency. I felt highly alert but, somehow, simultaneously rattled. I quickly called my boss as I was leaving the office, sobbing as I gave her my explanation for leaving work early. She could probably hardly hear me through my hyperventilating. I don't know why I felt it was necessary to call her at that exact moment while I was in such a rush; I was in shock.

As I drove to my granny's house, there were no thoughts; my mind went blank. The shock hadn't worn off. I felt as though I had taken a huge, deep breath and couldn't breathe out until I arrived at my destination. With both hands on the wheel, sat up particularly straighter than usual and with tense muscles, I exceeded the speed limit by an exceptional amount. Finally, I'd arrived. It wasn't time to breathe out just yet. I had to figure out what was going on.

I got there just in time – my mum and granny were getting in my mum's car, on their way to the hospital. Looks like Granny finally got a hold of Mum. As we drove, Granny explained everything. Well, I say everything – she explained as much as she knew… which wasn't a lot. It turns out, Grandpa was in Lidl doing the weekly food shop and collapsed. That's all we knew. He phoned Granny from his hospital bed and told her that the doctors said he's only got around three days to live. We were so confused. Granny said he was fine just this morning, going about his usual business.

For the rest of the drive, we travelled in silence. The shock had worn off, so my mind was chaos. *How could this be happening? How could our world turn upside down overnight?* My wonderful grandpa was the strong one. We weren't expecting this. It was usually Granny who was prone to taking unwell. For years, she had been in and out of the hospital for various conditions but always pushing through. Grandpa always seemed fine. *How could he go from fine to this? What's going on?*

I kept these thoughts to myself as we arrived at A&E. The hospital smelled of old people – that, along with a sharp tang of antiseptic. *Ding, ding, ding* played on a constant loop. This sound from what I assumed was the ECG machines sliced through our silence. It was irritating. We made a beeline for Grandpa's ward as directed by the receptionist. It was a huge room, filled with loads of other beds with elderly patients in them. I didn't have time to take it all in or notice our surroundings much – I had tunnel vision for Gramps.

He was sat up in bed with a huge smile. I wasn't expecting that. The doctors told us he had a stroke because his arteries hardened, making it difficult for his legs to get any oxygen, causing him to collapse outside of Lidl. He didn't look like someone who had just had a stroke. He seemed like his normal self. His normal self with a sentimental streak; he told us all multiple times about how much he loved us. This worried me. It wasn't like him – he'd usually show his love for us quicker than he'd declare it. We told the doctor about the "three days left to live" remarks that Grandpa had mentioned on the phone to Granny, hoping he had just gotten mixed up because of the stroke. The doctor confirmed that although they couldn't determine an exact timeline, things weren't looking good. They estimated three days, although they warned us it could be three weeks or three months; sometimes the unexpected happens and it could be hard for them to tell exactly. Most people in Grandpa's position would take this as a death sentence. Not Grandpa. He reassured us that he wasn't going anywhere. He kept repeating the mantra "mind over matter".

It turns out the phrase "mind over matter" wasn't just a mantra; I reckon it was a spell. At least for Grandpa, anyway. Months went by and Grandpa was still with us. So much for the "three days left to live" death sentence. Initially, Grandpa stayed with Granny. Carers would come in and out to look after him, but as Grandpa deteriorated, the family felt it would be best for him to stay at a care home, where he could access 24/7 support. Deteriorated is an understatement – to me, Grandpa almost became unrecognisable. He lost so much weight. My once tall, strong grandpa looked a fraction of his former self. Because of the stroke, in some ways, he didn't seem the same on the inside either. Don't get me wrong, in some ways he was very much the same: still thoughtful, still loved watching the wrestling, still delighted to see his family, still cracking silly jokes, still playing chess with me. However, there would be days where he seemed so disorientated and confused. I remember one day I went to visit, he was hallucinating and thought there was a little dog on his bed. I went along with it and patted the invisible dog, asking Gramps what his name was. Sometimes, you've got to have a laugh, especially with all the grief that comes from a situation like this. It's a strange feeling – grieving for someone who isn't dead yet. It feels like a heavy weight on your shoulders, an invisible stopwatch in your ear, a constant lump in your throat.

It was a heavy time. Just a few weeks after the hospital scare, I went through a messy break-up. Remember red-flag man? Yep – that's the one. I remember the night that Grandpa was told he'd have three days left to live. I was trying to sleep but I sobbed quietly to myself instead, and I couldn't stop. Red-flag man didn't comfort me, he didn't hold me; instead, he said, "Aimee, we're trying to sleep." That should have been the moment I kicked his sorry arse to the kerb. I've said it once and I'll say it again – hindsight is a wonderful thing. Despite being treated badly, I was still deeply heartbroken over the relationship ending. Regardless of how shitty a boyfriend he was, somehow he was my first love. That as well as seeing my grandpa on his deathbed made for a terrible year of grief and sadness.

Despite my sadness, Gramps still found a way to put a smile on my face whenever I would visit him. He'd introduce me to all the carers at his home, saying, "This is my granddaughter, Aimee! She's a dancer!" He would then proceed to boast about me with such pride, even when I was standing right there. It was a bit embarrassing, but it always touched me. He continued to repeat his "mind over matter" mantra, telling me how proud he was of his mindset – it had the power to defy what the doctor's thought was possible. I was equally impressed with his mind-over-matter spell. It was always something I believed in – the law of attraction and manifestation. I had no idea that my grandpa had a similar belief system.

I had spent years of my late teens and early twenties reading books and listening to podcasts such as *The Secret* by Rhonda Byrne and *The Bad B*tch Guide to Manifestation* by Maddie Cleary. Through these sources, and several others, I learnt that our deliberate thoughts and feelings can attract experiences into our lives. Studies show that when you believe you can do something, you are more likely to achieve it – similar to the placebo effect. Many self-help authors and podcasters claim that "like attracts like". This theory claims that if you focus your thoughts, energy and behaviours on what you want, you'll attract your desired outcome. They say to achieve this, you must have unwavering faith that what you want is already yours and act as though you already have it. So, for example, if you want a job promotion, you could think to yourself, what does that version of me, who already has the job, act like? What does she talk like? What does she walk like? What does she wear to work? What time does she get up in the morning? What does she do in her free time? Then, to manifest the job promotion, you could start embodying these behaviours, kind of like method acting.

A big part of this process is gratitude practice: being thankful for everything in your life, no matter how big or small, no matter how real or imaginary. I hadn't practised gratitude in a while, but Grandpa's mind-over-matter mindset reminded me to give it another go. I used to sit every morning with a notepad and pen, writing lists of all the things I was grateful for. I would then read the list out loud and take a few minutes to deeply think about why I was grateful for these things. Most things on the list were real, but some of those things were made up – an attempt to manifest my goals. I noticed that my mood, well-being and confidence drastically improved whenever I implemented gratitude into my morning routine.

Don't get me wrong, as with anything in life, these theories have their critics. For some of the law of attraction concepts, there is no or little scientific evidence to support them. Also, some people view the law of attraction as toxic positivity. I can see how it could be interpreted in this way, and I certainly wouldn't want anyone to feel triggered by it. So, what I would say in response is, if you want to give it a go, make it work for you. Make your own rules if you need to. For example, if I have negative thoughts or feelings, I don't try to force myself out of it or feel guilty for it. Sometimes, I try to move on and quickly switch my mindset, but for other times, that's just not realistic or helpful. Often, we need to sit in the hard feelings – that's a big part of being human. I remind myself that as humans, we have a range of emotions for a reason, and feeling down doesn't mean that we are negative people. So, I let myself marinade in the hard feelings, and then, when I'm ready, I try to use the law of attraction to work its magic. I rarely force it.

Some recovery and psychology websites claim that the law of attraction can be used to help those in recovery. For example, the website The Process Recovery Center suggests that the law of attraction can help addicts manifest happiness from within, which could help them abstain from seeking external happiness or escapism in the form of drugs or alcohol. The website Enlightened Recovery recommends the use of affirmations to support recovery. This involves constant thinking and saying pre-planned mantras to help manifest the desired goals. For example, "I am healing," or, "I am at peace." I wonder if my grandpa used the law of attraction to overcome his addition issues, all those years ago. I wonder if that's how mind over matter started.

The Secret tells stories of people who were terminally ill manifesting their way to being healed. I couldn't believe that Grandpa was one of those people. Knowing this made me feel even more connected to Grandpa than I already was.

18

How Childhood Affects Adulthood

Many months had passed since Grandpa's hospital scare. Although I frequently went to visit him, sometimes I forgot about Granny. It could be tricky to balance everything – with full-time work, visiting Grandpa, hitting the gym, maintaining a social life and trying to get back out there in the dating world. It was a lot. I felt guilty about not making enough time for her; I imagined that she would have been lonely. So, with a heavy heart, I paid her a visit.

For once, I wasn't yapping on about the prison. We were discussing the parent and baby dance classes I facilitated in addition to my work with nursery and lower primary school pupils. During lockdown, I researched early years development, so it became a great area of interest. I can't remember why I got talking to my gran about this – it seems a bit random. She was probably the only person who'd been willing to listen. The rest of my family thought I talked too much. Not my granny though; she always made time for me. She was also grateful for the distraction, given everything that was happening with Grandpa. She wanted our conversations to feel natural and normal. This comforted her.

Five minutes into the conversation, my gran recited a famous quote I had never heard before: "Give me the child until he is seven and I'll give you the man" – Francis Xavier. This quote articulates the significance of our early years' experiences and how these experiences can have the most powerful influence on the person we become.

What has this got to do with a book about young prisoners? I'm sure by now you've realised how it's all linked. Especially after the chapters around ACEs and trauma. However, I'd like to dive a little deeper in this chapter, and funnily enough, some of the young men I've met in prison have shown interest in diving deeper within this topic too.

It was a usual Tuesday in the prison. We were having a gab at the start of class, welcoming a new participant, Michael. Michael was giving us a little background on his life – a little too much, actually. We learnt so much about him in just five minutes, I was struggling to find a polite way to ask him to rein it in, especially because it was his first week, so I didn't want to discourage him. He told us how he had four children, all to different mums. I couldn't believe it; he looked like a child himself.

Forty minutes into the two-hour session and it was time for a tea break. Michael got chatting about his wee ones again. He talked about them with such pride and awe. He then went on to discuss the parenting class that he attended within the prison.

"I go to that too; it's been really good," Kieran said, interrupting Michael mid-sentence. Michael didn't seem to mind. They bounced off of one another, telling the group what they'd learnt so far.

"They say the first five years of life is most important for brain development – int that mad? Like, even before they can walk or talk or that, they're taking in so much of the world. I used to think what happened in those years didn't matter," Michael explained.

Kieran agreed, "Aye, me an' all. What's that attachment thingy we learnt about again?"

"The attachment theory?" I asked.

"Aye, that's the one. I enjoyed learning that. Blew ma mind."

We talked a little about what the attachment theory is, but we didn't get too deep. The non-parents of the group swiftly changed the subject and then break time was over. I remember feeling so impressed and relieved that the young parents in prison were undertaking this significant learning.

The attachment theory claims that a strong bond between parent and child, in the first few years of life, is crucial for the child's brain development. If a child has a strong bond with a parent or carer, they are considered to have a secure attachment style. People who are securely attached are usually more trusting and connected with others. They aren't afraid to explore the world, as they know they have a safe base which they can return to at any time. When the connection between the main carer and the child is weak, the child will have an insecure attachment style. There are several types of insecure attachment. In general, insecurely attached people tend to have difficulty forming relationships due to lack of social skills and trust issues.

Our attachment style is formed at an age where we are too young to articulate our anguish. In cases of insecure attachment in infants, stress responses can be triggered frequently, leading to elevated levels of cortisol and adrenaline. Over time, repeated exposure to such stress – known as toxic stress – can impair brain development and disrupt the immune system. In fact, prolonged toxic stress during early life may even alter how genes are expressed, with long-term consequences for both mental and physical health.

A thirty-five-year follow-up study of Harvard students found a striking link between childhood relationships and health in midlife. Among those who did not describe their relationship with their mothers as warm, 91% had been diagnosed with serious diseases such as hypertension, coronary heart disease, ulcers, or alcoholism. By comparison, less than half of those with warm maternal relationships had such diagnoses (Russek and Schwartz, 1997). Similarly, researchers at the University of Minnesota used the attachment theory to predict school dropout rates. By observing children as young as age three, they were able to predict with 77% accuracy which students would eventually leave school before graduation (Sprouts, 2018).

In the first three years of life, our brains are changing and adapting to the world around us, more so than at any other age. Babies' brains will develop in accordance with what they're exposed to. Doctor Suzanne Zeedyk gives an example of this in an Education Scotland YouTube video titled *Pre-Birth to Three: Doctor Suzanne Zeedyk – Brain Development.* In the video, she claims that when a baby is exposed to a home where there is a lot of violence, to survive they must develop a brain which is equipped to deal with violence. They do this through constantly inspecting their environment, checking for danger. Their brain will learn how to produce cortisol quickly and in immense amounts. We all need cortisol at times of high pressure. However, if we have cortisol in our brains all the time, it is not good for us. Cortisol is meant to help us deal with urgent, dangerous stress, such as escaping from a predator. So, when we have a child who's had a difficult morning before school, immersed in a violent environment at home, they may feel the same stress response in their bodies as someone who has escaped from a dangerous predator. How can we expect them to sit still at school? How can we expect them to listen? Their brain will now always look for danger. If they are spending so much energy looking for danger, it will be more difficult for them to learn and to build relationships. It will be more difficult for them to learn empathy and to let go of mistrust, even as an adult.

An adult or child who struggles with empathy and trust is more at risk of hurting others. A child who struggles to trust others and build connections may be missing positive role models and good influences. A child who cannot concentrate in school, due to subconsciously scanning their environment for threat, may get frustrated; they may misbehave. Their education is affected, even into secondary school. They might then leave school with no prospects. How do they make money with a lack of social skills and no qualifications? Drug dealing? Stealing? Something worse? Based on the experiences they're exposed to, what kind of brain are we asking our children to form?

19

Dubbing the Door

Michael was settling in well with our core group of boys – Brandy, Kieran, and Gary. We had other members who would come and go, but they weren't able to commit. It turns out, the boys who liked to take part in activities were always being pulled in different directions. A lot of things seemed to clash with their dance slot: visits, work parties, exams at education. We were hoping we'd have a chance to recruit new members soon enough.

Until then, we persisted with our small core group. It was a summer's day, although you would be none the wiser down at the performing-arts space. There were no windows, and the room was quite dark. We had a full house, apart from a missing newbie from the week before. Brandy also hadn't arrived yet, but we knew about that. The week before, he told us how he'd be late because he had to meet with his lawyer before the session.

"Guys, we're trying to recruit for some new members. Do you know anyone who might be interested in joining the group?" I asked hopefully.

"Ehh, no' really. Other than maybe Brandon," one of the younger prisoners responded. He was quite new to the group, so he didn't realise that Brandy was a long-time regular.

"Who the fuck is Brandon?" Michael asked.

"Brandy?!" I replied in a high pitched, surprised tone. The way I said his name sounded more like a question than a statement.

Michael laughed and nodded with realisation. "Awk, he's been coming down for ages," Michael added. Brandy's ears must have been burning; he entered the room right on cue.

"Guys, where's Paul? I thought he really enjoyed it last week?" I asked while I set up the music.

"He's dubbing his door. Shitebag," Brandy replied.

The rest of the boys laughed, and some bitching about the newbie kicked off. Brandy's mean-girl tone took me by surprise. He and Paul seemed to get along so well; I couldn't imagine Brandy saying this to Paul's face. I didn't know what "dubbing the door" meant, but I made an educated guess and assumed it was something to do with locking up the cell door and not coming out. I was right.

"He's got enemies and he's been too feart to deal with them," Kieran explained.

"Never dub yer door! Just don't do it. People will think they can walk all over ye when ye come oot," Gary added.

"Right, guys, that's enough. Stop talking about Paul like that!" Sam interjected. She was always able to put them in their place when she saw behaviours she didn't like. We began the dance class, and all mention of Paul was forgotten about.

It got to tea-break time when Michael approached me with some ideas. He pulled out a scrap piece of paper from his joggers and began reading from it.

"Ashley Banjo's new TV show on Channel 4, 7pm tomorrow night." He looked up from his paper. "Have ye seen the advert?"

I shook my head.

"Well, he's training up dance crews from around the UK. Looks sick, man." His enthusiasm was quite sweet, to be honest.

"I'll definitely give it a watch and let you know what I think. Thanks for letting me know," I replied warmly, even though I didn't intend on watching it. My Freeview wasn't working at home, but I could still watch Netflix, thankfully. It still baffled me that the boys got TV in prison.

"I was also thinking up suggestions of themes we could do for our new dance," Michael added before breaking eye contact to read from his sheet again. "Dance through the decades. *Step Up* movie. Salsa dance."

I tried my best not to laugh as he handed over the piece of paper. Instead, I praised him for his initiative and explained how I'd show Sam during our lunch break.

Tea break was over, so we continued with our contemporary dance. Sam had choreographed it, and the boys loved it. I never would have expected to teach contemporary in the prison, but Sam had a way to make it cool and gritty. The routine consisted of punchy arm swings, huge jumps, and floor work. The song we used was "Radioactive" by Imagine Dragons.

After rehearsing the dance, we set a creative task – the boys had to work in small teams to create the next part of the routine. We asked them to mix up their favourite moves from the dance, placing them in a different order. By the end of the class, we combined this with Sam's choreography. We were able to watch them perform the dance from start to finish, without our help. Brandon was at the front. He knew it inside out, and he had good rhythm. He was carrying the others through; they all copied him. Well, everyone apart from Gary – he was making weird eye contact with me again. It creeped me out. I avoided watching him at all costs. Michael had missed a lot of the routine, since he was a new start. He did well to catch up in such a brief time. Kieran was bouncing around in the background, singing along to the music. It came to the end of the dance, and he dramatically limped away from the dance floor, complaining about his sore foot. No wonder they called him the poster boy of youth theatre.

We had five minutes of class left. We gathered the group to form a circle, and they followed my cool-down routine, consisting of different stretches.

"Number oot a ten?" Brandy asked as Sam stopped the music.

We asked everyone our usual check-out question before packing up our things. We all stood around, close to the door, waiting for our prison officer in the glass box to escort the boys back to their halls. As we waited for our officer to get the all-clear via his radio, there was more time for chit-chat. Once again, the conversation revolved around the newbie who was dubbing his door.

"A mean, he can't dub his door forever. It's ages until he gets out so it's no' like he could even do this for a short time before being released." Brandon sighed.

I tried my best to change the subject. "Brandon, when do you get out?"

"You'll know when I'm released, sweetheart. You'll get a Facebook friend request from me."

I smiled. "Sorry, Brandon, but I won't be accepting."

"Wit? You need to. I'll keep it on the DL, a promise!"

"No!" I replied while laughing.

"I still want to dance when I get out. I'll call up the prison and ask. I'll even start a wee Facebook Live, telling everyone I need Aimee from the jail to teach me some *Footloose*."

My laughter amplified, and with that, the rest of the boys cracked up too. A few weeks before, Brandon had mentioned how he loved the *Footloose* movie reboot. Mainly because he fancied the lead actor, Julianne Hough. At the time, I told him it was one of my favourite movies too and how I learnt the line-dance routine that's featured in it. I had warmed up to Brandy so much that I even told him why I had learnt the line dance – Red-flag man asked me to learn it so I could teach him it in our earlier stages of dating. Looking back, I can't believe I told Brandy about this. I didn't hear the end of it after that. Every week, he would pester me to try and get us all to learn it in the class. The rest of the boys were not so keen, so we couldn't make it happen. Majority rules. Brandon seemed gutted, but this didn't stop him from freestyling his version of the line-dance moves during his creative task. He didn't seem to notice that his country steps didn't exactly match the vibe of Sam's expressive, serious contemporary dance.

Our prison officer was finally ready to escort the boys to their hall. We walked with them down the narrow corridors.

Brandon occasionally jumped up and swung from the handlebars on the ceiling, showing off, until the prison officer gave him a telling-off. The sun beamed through a row of arched gothic windows as we walked. I was instantly reminded it was a summer's day. I was surprised that the corridors were decorated with such vibrant colour; it's not how I imagined a prison would look at all. There was also artwork and poems on the walls, created by the inmates. A lot of it was very impressive. We got to a T-junction and so we parted ways with our group. We said goodbye with our usual knuckle punch, then Sam and I made our way to reception.

We handed our visitor passes to the officer behind the desk and informed them we'd be back after lunch. As soon as we got outside, I had to squint my eyes. The bright sun felt intense, especially after being in that dark room all morning. Our chat circulated back to Paul.

"Imagine it getting that bad you feel you can't ever leave your cell. Think of how scared you'd have to be to go to those lengths." Sam frowned while shaking her head.

"I know. I think it's easy for us to forget how hard it must be for the boys. We see them having fun and letting their guard down. We only see that because we create a safe environment for them."

"Think how bad it must be for your mental health if you were to dub the door all the time."

"You know, I was surprised at the boys for talking about Paul like that. I really saw a different side to them today."

After lunch, we got chatting about this same topic with one of the prison officers, Stewart. He explained how he sees a completely different side to the boys in performing arts.

"They're like different people up in the hall. Tryna be the big man. I've seen Kieran go off his nut, attacking randoms for no reason."

Sam nodded in agreement. "Yeah, I can see that wee side of him. I can imagine him kicking off. Remember Stephen? Same with him. He seemed sweet enough in the dance class, but I could imagine him being the silent deadly type."

I shook my head. "No way. I can't imagine them like that. Am I just being naive?"

"Nah, it's easily done. But both those boys have real rage issues," Stewart warned.

"I wonder why they've not kicked off in dance?"

"They've not had a reason to," Stewart responded.

A million questions engulfed my brain. I tried my best to express my burning curiosity.

"Do you think when the boys are in our class, acting differently than normal, they are putting on an act? Or do you think they are just able to be vulnerable and show parts of their personality they'd never usually let loose?" I asked, knowing full well which answer I wanted to hear.

After a short pause to think, Stewart answered: "I think a bit of both."

20

Gender Stereotypes

In the space of one week, we managed to get some taster sessions in the diary. It was time to recruit some new members. Sam was asked to deliver on another project, so I was flying solo. As I drove to the prison, "I Love It" by Icona Pop came on the radio. I sobbed as it reminded me of my grandpa. As I drove and listened to the song, I had an instant flashback to that day when Grandpa surprised me through singing that same song so randomly. It was so funny at the time and embodied Grandpa's happy, playful spirit.

It had been a while since I went out on my own, but I was feeling confident and excited as I arrived at the prison. My optimism started to shrink as I chatted with the youth work team. They seemed nervous for me. They walked me down to the games hall, where the taster sessions would take place.

"Listen, Aimee, I don't know how this is gonna work out. I can't imagine many of them joining in."

Their negativity was frustrating. I tried to let it pass, but I was beginning to feel anxious. The boys usually had a gym slot at that time, so the youth work team thought it would be best for me to come to them, pitching the class as a workout session rather than a dance class. There were still so many stereotypes around dance, so this seemed like a smart approach.

As I entered the games hall, a group of inmates were already there, kicking a football around and carrying on. There was around fifteen of them, which was quite intimidating. I was used to working with groups of this size only when it came to children, never in the prison. I had a nervous stomach. To get their attention, the prison officer on duty whistled loudly before motioning for them to come over and sit down.

"Right, boys, we've got this lovely young lady here to lead a workout session with you. Show some respect, be on your best behaviour, and listen up."

They were silent, but they looked unimpressed. I noticed that Gary was part of the group, although he never made eye contact with me (for a change). I went along with it, pretending not to know him; I didn't want to cramp his style. I introduced myself and explained what I'd be taking them through. Usually I'd be much chattier, trying to get to know them and making small talk first, but my nerves got the better of me. I felt like I went back in time to my very first day in the prison, all those years ago, but worse. To mask my nerves, I decided it would be best to keep the intro short and sweet.

Next, I got on with the warm-up. I blasted GBX on the speaker and started running on the spot, asking the boys to copy before moving on to star jumps. Most of them were laughing already and not joining in fully. I ignored it and kept going. *Oh no*: a few boys walked away and sat out. And another few. And another few. By the end of the song, everyone was gone, even Gary (what a traitor!). The boys were taken out of the gym hall and to the weightlifting gym next door.

"Don't worry, pal; this was to be expected," the officer on duty reassured me while patting my back. I could feel my cheeks turning pink; I was so embarrassed. I felt like such a failure. I had to hold back my tears. He could probably tell I wasn't in the mood for chit-chat, so he carried on, filling the awkward silence.

"They didn't even know you were coming today. We arranged it so last-minute. They thought they were coming down for their gym session, but we sprung this on them."

This made me feel a little better. They probably felt that the class was being forced on them; they weren't given a choice. That's not right. They reacted on instinct; it wasn't personal. Despite this realisation, I was so hard on myself for the rest of the day. My realisation was silent. I was yet to speak. As I bent down to switch my speaker off, I felt a tear trickle down my face. I wiped it away subtly, hoping the officer wouldn't notice.

He was clearly oblivious as he rambled on and on. "I think it's because you introduced yourself as a dance teacher. If I were you, I'd leave the dance part completely out. It puts them off."

Back then, when I was upset, there was only one person who could make me feel better. So that evening, I paid my gran a visit. I filled her in on the whole story.

"I think that prison officer's right, hen. They hear the word dance and they don't want to know. They just need to learn to accept and be unashamed of their feminine side. They need to learn it's OK not to be macho."

I could tell my gran meant well, but this response is part of the problem. Who said that dance is feminine? Who said that dance isn't manly? Dance shouldn't be gendered. It isn't gendered. That's just a label that society puts on it. Colours don't have a gender; sports don't have a gender; music doesn't either. The list goes on. We've placed gender onto these things. When parents attempt to force this socially constructed idea onto their children, it changes how they see the world and the experiences they're exposed to.

A few weeks prior, I had attended a training session at a primary school. One of the teachers told me how impressed she had been with a little boy in her class. He had been very resistant at first, but after a few weeks, he absolutely loved dance class and gave it 100% effort. The teacher decided to call his parents to express how well he was getting on. She was met with concern. The parents didn't want him taking part in dance. They didn't need to convey their reasoning; their tone was noticeably clear. The teacher calmy explained what was involved in the session, describing how different the dance class was to the mainstream stereotypes. In other words, she had to reassure them that the dance class wasn't girly or feminine. She shouldn't have had to over-explain herself or to justify the dance class. Yes, her dance class was completely different to the usual stereotypes of dance. But so what if it hadn't been?

21

The Homelessness Crisis

Although our taster sessions didn't go to plan, we remained hopeful that we'd have a decent turnout for our next session. In the morning that followed, Sam and I sat at the comfortable chairs and tables at the back of the performing-arts room. I filled Sam in on the mortifying mishap from the day before while she did her best to reassure me it could happen to anyone. We moved on to recapping our lesson plan when two unfamiliar faces walked in. They looked very young, around eighteen or nineteen years old, I'd say.

"Hi, my name's Aimee; this is Sam." I smiled warmly at them both as they approached us. They still looked half asleep. They smiled politely and took a seat next to us.

"Alrighty, I'm Tony." Tony was the shorter of the two. He had clean-cut facial hair and extremely short, blond hair on his head.

"I'm Marc." Marc was slightly taller and looked a little older, but not by much. He was slim but he also looked filled out and broad. He had acne scars on his face; it was a reminder of how young they were. I had a brief flashback to my unfortunate teenage acne days. How glad I was that phase of life had passed.

"So, do you know why you're here?" Sam asked.

"Naw!" Tony replied while laughing nervously.

"Eh, performing arts? Music 'n' that?" Marc asked while he lifted a guitar from the wall and began fiddling with the strings.

The prison officer on shift poked her head out of the glass office and motioned for Marc to put the guitar down.

"No, you're here for dance!" I explained.

"Wit, ceilidh dancing 'n' that?" Tony asked.

Sam and I reassured our new recruits that they would not be doing the Gay Gordons together any time soon. We gave a brief introduction to our classes so they knew what to expect going forward. We also tried to get to know our new participants. We found out that exercise and the gym was not of any interest to Tony; he'd rather be in bed. Marc seemed more enticed by the idea of a workout, but his legs were sore from his gym session the day before. We had our work cut out for us. Sam was mid-sentence when Brandy walked in with a spring in his step.

"What time do you call this?" she asked jokingly.

Brandy welcomed our newbies before explaining why he was late. He then went on to justify why our usual members hadn't made an appearance. Some were at education, some had a visit, and, in Brandy's words, some just "couldn't be arsed".

With that, we started our session with a check-in question.

"Number oot a ten?" Brandy asked smugly. Both Marc and Tony shot him a confused dose of side eye.

"Nope, we're going to try a new check-in question today. A bit of an icebreaker," I explained. "If you were an animal, what would you be and why? Chose two. You could then combine their names together. For example, I think I would be a…" I paused for a few seconds to think. "I think I'd be a squirrel and a dolphin."

"So, you'd be a sqolphin?" Sam asked with amusement.

"Why a squirrel? 'Cause of your big cheeks?" Brandy added.

I burst out laughing while telling him off. My laughter gave the others the go-ahead to giggle too. The icebreaker lasted around five minutes. Sam chose a budgie because she liked to talk a lot, and Brandon chose a dog because he's loyal. I can't remember their second choices, but their new animal hybrid names made for some good entertainment. Tony chose a sloth. This was a clear protest to any form of physical activity. Despite that, he joined in with the warm-up, reluctantly so.

After the warm-up, we let the guys stop for water. Brandon filled up a jug of diluting juice and offered it around the room, giving everyone a refill.

"I'm fucked!" Tony complained.

"Aye, my legs are feeling it," Marc chimed in.

"Come on, guys, shake what ya mamma gave ya!" Brandon tried his best to motivate our newbies, but he was met with hesitancy.

In the end, we resorted to bribery. "We've brought in biscuits. How about we do twenty minutes more and then we'll have a tea break?" I asked persuasively.

"Hmm. Ten more minutes?" Tony haggled. It was more of a statement than a question. I couldn't get over how hard he was to motivate.

"Fifteen more minutes and that's that." Sam asserted her dominance while simultaneously using a friendly tone of voice.

Next, we taught a basic street dance. We used a song that the guys requested. It was Macklemore's "And We Danced". It was such a feel-good song, which helped to create a great atmosphere. There was part of the dance where the group had to take four walks forwards and four walks backwards. On their fourth walk, they had to use their arms to create their own movement or shape. Brandon hit a thumbs-up pose while holding a cheesy smile as if he was posing for a family portrait. He looked so wholesome, corny, and innocent in that moment; I found it hilarious. Marc linked his hands together to create a love-heart shape which he held high above his head and looked up, as if he was at a Taylor Swift concert. Tony didn't do much with his arms at all; he was just trying to get the feet right. I noticed how Brandon smiled constantly. He looked as though he was really enjoying himself. I then realised that I also couldn't stop smiling for the whole session. I felt so buzzed with amusement, laughter, and job satisfaction. This was the happiest I had felt in a long time, especially with everything going on at home. Premature grief for my grandpa gave me what felt like a permanent heavy heart, but these guys knew how to lighten the load.

After a few practices, we taught one last piece of choreography. We asked the guys to bend their knees, one at a time, as if someone was behind them, pushing the back of their kneecaps forwards. They then had to contract their stomach muscles as if they'd been punched, while placing their hands on their thighs. Finally, we asked them to imagine they had a pencil sticking out from their chest. We got them to move side to side, leading with their chest, as if they were drawing a smiley face in the air. Brandon practised the moves repeatedly, getting quicker every time. He was showing off how quickly he had picked it up through demonstrating it to the class while chanting, "Chicken leg, chicken leg, smiley face!"

When we'd finished teaching the choreography, I gave everyone a high five and praised individuals for their specific achievements.

"Shall we try that one more time, without Aimee and me? Can we watch?" Sam asked.

"Nah," Tony responded defiantly. We soon realised he would just answer in this way no matter what. He'd go to the negative response habitually. But he always joined in, nonetheless.

After the last dance, we sat back at the comfy chairs for biscuits and juice. After reflecting on the dance session, we chatted away.

"So, Tony, Marc, tell us more about yourselves! What was life like before you came in here?" I asked with an animated tone. I had a brief flashback of how differently I used to speak when I first started teaching in the prison. I almost couldn't believe how bold I was to ask such a question, and with such confidence. I felt like a different person sometimes.

"Well, I was homeless for four year," Tony responded with ease. "Ma maw kicked me out when I was fifteen."

I was appalled. I suddenly remembered why I'd usually stick to the safer questions like, "What's for dinner tonight?"

"I'm so sorry to hear that. That must've been incredibly tough."

"No, not really. It was OK. The hardest part was looking for homeless shelters with available beds."

"But you were only fifteen; surely something should've been done about that?" I responded in disbelief.

He shrugged and changed the subject. As the group continued their conversation, I thought about Tony's upbringing and felt a huge wave of sadness for him. *No wonder he ended up in here*, I thought. *Three meals a day and a roof over your head. Doesn't sound so bad when you consider the alternative.*

"What about you, Marc? What was life like before prison?" Sam asked.

"Awk, a wis doin' good oot there, man; am just in for something daft," Marc began before explaining the different jobs he did and where he lived before. As Marc went on, I glanced at the clock and realised we still had ten minutes left. The session felt much longer than usual. Probably because we cut the dance part short due to Tony's bargaining skills. The conversation took a natural turn, and we were on to a lighter topic.

"What's everyone watching on TV just now?" Sam asked.

"Nothing, there's fuck all on," Tony responded in a monotone manner. His lack of enthusiasm was not personal to the dance class at least.

"Well, I'm watching *Euphoria* and *Screw*. Finished them both with—" Sam was mid-sentence when Brandon interjected.

"Shhhh! No spoilers; I've still got three episodes of each to go!"

"Yous have it good in here with your TV options. I was teaching at a secure unit the other day and they were telling me sometimes they get sent to their rooms for hours with no TV, no phone, nothing to keep them entertained." I thought it was about time I contributed to the conversation. I had spent a good chunk of time silently pondering Tony's homeless teenage years.

"Aye, that's 'cause they would have done something wrong and that wis their punishment," Brandy explained. "Happened to me when I was in residential. Thank fuck I never ended up in secure; they've got it worse. They tried to take me there hunners of times but they couldny."

"Why?" I asked, realising we couldn't keep the conversation surface-level for much longer.

"I'd bolt. I was missing for two and a half months. They all thought a wis deed."

"Where did you go?" Sam asked.

"All over. When you know how to wangle the train system, you can go anywhere for free." He went on to describe in detail how he'd trick the ScotRail staff and get through the barriers for free without being caught.

"I've never been in secure either," Marc stated. "Why were they trying to send you there anyway?"

"A wis committing armed robbery at aged thirteen, holding people up in shops 'n' that."

Brandon's statement floored me. Thirteen years old. What? How does that even happen? I couldn't help myself; the words left my mouth before I had time to filter them.

"But… you were soooo young!" I blurted out more slowly than usual. "Why do you think that happened… at that age?" As soon as the words left my mouth, I realised I was prying, and I worried it was inappropriate or unprofessional. I just couldn't believe it.

For once, Brandon's response wasn't in the form of entertainment or class-clown behaviour. He looked as though he was thinking deeply.

"Well, I tried drink and drugs for the first time when I was seven or eight. My older brother would steal ma da's smoke box and bottle of booze. He'd make me tan half of it so that way a couldny grass. But it backfired on him 'cause it's what made me become pals wae all of his mates. When I got a bit older, I'd be out smoking and drinking wae them all. I'd be gaggin' for a drink all the time. So, aye, that's probably how it happened. I ended up getting in trouble with my bro's older pals all the time. Social work was always on ma back."

Brandon was talking for a fair bit without the others piping in, which was an unusual circumstance in the prison. Maybe because Tony and Marc were a few years younger; it was probably a respect thing.

Brandon carried on without a pause. "I even stole a car when I was ten years old. I was cruising down the scheme at fifteen miles an hour, thinking I was the big man." His tone became slightly more vibrant as he started laughing with Marc and Tony. He wasn't laughing in an insensitive way; it was more as if he was mocking his younger self. "I was at high school for only six weeks before a wis banned fae all mainstream high schools in the city."

Brandon's monologue eventually came to a natural end. As the group got ready to go, we asked if they had any requests for dance styles or music for future sessions.

"Aye, a want that Aimee to teach us some *Footloose*!" Brandon asserted.

"Yeah, but everyone's got to say yes to that idea if you want it to happen. It's not the Brandy show!" I couldn't believe that he was still harping on about line dancing. What an unusual request from a young man.

"I'll get them all to say yes. Won't I, boys?" He was relentless. Marc and Tony nodded tentatively, clearly unaware of what they were signing up to.

I finally gave in. "OK, OK, next time then."

"Why do you like it so much anyway?" Sam asked in amusement.

"It's that Julianne Hough, the main lassie. She gets ma motor goin'…"

Brandon's *Footloose* fantasy was interrupted through the prison officer calling the boys towards the door. She was ready to escort them back to the hall. Each one of them said thank you and initiated a fist pump before leaving, even Tony.

When I got home from work that night, I kept thinking about Tony. I knew that homelessness was a problem in Scotland; I just never considered that it was a problem for children in Scotland. As usual, I got the laptop out and did some digging.

I found that in 2023, over 16,000 children in Scotland were part of households assessed as homeless. That's forty-five children a day – according to the Shelter Scotland website. Even more shocking was how many were living in temporary accommodation. By March 2023, nearly 9,600 children were stuck in limbo, living in places that were never meant to be permanent.

What angered me most was learning that some families, even with a legal right to housing, weren't given a place to stay. This practice, called 'gatekeeping', saw at least 445 households denied temporary accommodation that they should've had by law. Shelter Scotland found that even when a place was offered, it often wasn't fit to live in. In over 3,500 cases, the accommodation was deemed legally "unsuitable". This means it didn't meet even the most basic standards.

The system's failing, and the longer it drags on, the more children fall through the cracks – just like Tony did.

22

Second Chances

One of the hardest parts of watching my grandpa dying was watching my mum watching him die. The spell cast using mind over matter truly worked, and Grandpa lived for one whole year after the doctors gave him three days left to live. He was a fighter. Although it felt miraculous, it was the worst year of my life. I moved back in with my family a few months before he passed away – I felt it was important to be with them, especially for Mum. I also found it tough being in the flat on my own, with everything going on.

I felt lucky to be back living with my family. They lived in a four-bedroom new-build house on a quiet estate in a small town. It was significantly bigger, much more modern, and flashier than the house we grew up in as kids. It was also much warmer than the wee flat I had just moved out of. I was so grateful for that, as someone who feels the cold easily. It was just my mum and dad in the house – my sister had already flown the nest a few years ago; she was living with her boyfriend. Unlike me, she wasn't a boomerang that somehow kept coming back.

My parents worked hard for everything they had. My dad was an executive head chef, so we grew up watching him do crazy sixteen-hour shifts, hardly getting a day off. It was an intense industry to be part of, so when my dad would get home from work, he'd want to switch off completely and not talk about his day. My mum worked as a PA at a college in Glasgow. She worked closely with the vice principle – minuting meetings, organising events and undertaking other administrative duties. When she was a child, she envisioned a job that had something to do with animals. She loved animals so much. She grew up next to a farm, where she'd get to look after and ride the horses. She also had her own sheepdog that she adored, as well as many bunny rabbits which she named after the planets. She tells me that's why she was always so supportive of my dance career, despite it being seen by some as an unstable, unpredictable job. When it came to her own career, she wished that she had the opportunities as a young person to follow her knowing (as Glennon Doyle would say). So, when I told Mum that I wanted to go to dance college, she told me to go for it and that life was too short not to.

My sister and I had a great childhood. Looking back, I'm very aware of how lucky and privileged we were. Mum and Dad took us on family holidays and family days out, we had birthday parties, and we were frequently allowed to have our friends from school over. My parents had a lovely relationship that we admired. I've always been grateful that I had a healthy, loving marriage modelled for me as a child. We all got on well growing up. Despite this, as I became a young adult, our relationships felt strained as we argued a lot. It felt as though we were always butting heads over something, and it could escalate quickly. I think that my mum and I were too similar, so we often clashed – both sensitive, both fiery. This was one of the reasons I moved out to my wee flat in the first place. Moving back in with them meant I had to work hard on this, especially with all the premature, overwhelming grief we were feeling for my grandpa, my mum's dad.

As expected, my mum struggled a lot with my grandpa's illness. During the day, she'd appear as a hard shell, like nothing could touch her. But at night, I'd hear her crying herself to sleep. My heart ached for her. I wished there was something I could do to take her pain away. I did what I could to help – visiting Grandpa in the care home as much as I could. This took some of the pressure off Mum. We bonded because of this, and during this time, my mum always told me how grateful she was for me stepping up. She'd say that we were a great team.

One night, I overheard my mum crying alone in her room while Dad was still at work. I chapped on the door and, when given the go-ahead, crawled into bed beside her. As I hugged her, I asked her what was wrong.

"Oh, nothing. You know, just thinking about Grandpa." She flashed a fake smile to mask her sorrow. She didn't fool me – I could see the hurt behind her eyes. A daughter knows.

"Mum, it seems like it's more than just that. You can tell me anything, remember."

"I'm just thinking about Grandpa's life. I don't want to tell you too much. I don't want you to see Grandpa differently while he's still with us."

Despite being instantly concerned, I put on a brave face. "Mum, I won't see him differently. I already know he was an alcoholic, and you've told me stories about how he could be at his worst while drinking. But you know how much I love him anyway. I'm always advocating for the prisoners in my class; I don't judge them, so why do you think I'd judge my grandpa?" I smiled softly, trying to reassure her to open up.

"You know I love your grandpa so much. But this year has brought back a lot of hard memories that I haven't thought about in forever..." As Mum went on, pre-empting the inevitable blow, I could see how many trips down memory lane she had been taking. I guess it must be natural, when someone you've known forever is dying, to think about their life – the good and the bad times.

"There were times when we'd hear your grandpa coming home from a bender, so we'd hide Granny in the bedroom wardrobe." When she said "we", she was referring to herself as well as her older brother and sister. "He'd look all over the house for her and ask us where she was, and we'd say we didn't know. We were so scared."

I was stunned. In the past, my mum had mentioned how they had a difficult home life when Grandpa was drinking, but I didn't realise how terrified they all were. How was this the same man who collected thoughtful gifts for us at car boot sales and thought of cheesy songs for me to play in my dance classes?

"There was one time where we tried to leave him. Granny packed our bags and off we went when he was sleeping. But Granny forgot her purse." She said that last part with despair, as if she was reliving the memory as she told it. "We needed her purse – it was a different time. We obviously couldn't use technology to pay for things like how we can today. We needed money for the bus. So, Granny sent your uncle in to climb through the window, to try and get it. I was terrified for him."

Mum never finished that story before starting the next one. I didn't interrupt; I could tell she needed to get all this off her chest. How did I get to my mid-twenties without hearing my mum talk about this honestly in depth?

"Mum, did Grandpa ever physically hurt you?" I asked hesitantly.

"Yes." She screwed up her face as if she could remember exactly how much it hurt, as if it was yesterday. I could tell it was painful for her to continue, but she did. "He was very violent to all of us. I feel ashamed to admit it. I remember one time I left home when I was about sixteen. I'd had enough – so I ran away and stayed at a friend's house. I went back to collect my things, and I heard him come in. He was so, so drunk. So, I hid under the bed while I waited for him to leave. The sweat was pouring down me – just from pure fear. I knew he would have been so angry and scary if he found me."

I started to taste my salty tears with a lump in my throat. I pictured my mum as a harmless, frightened young girl, and the lump thickened. I felt protective of my mum's inner child.

"Grandpa was a good dad when he wasn't drinking, you know." Her voice rose an octave when she spoke, as she let out a small cry. It seemed to cause her just as much pain reliving the good memories as it did the bad.

"I have memories of him buying me apple turnovers at the weekend and him taking me to work with him. I must have been about seven. It was quality father-daughter time.

I loved it." She started to genuinely smile through her tears. "I also remember how he'd help me rescue birds that had been hurt. He made them shelter and gave them food and water. He loved my wee dog, too, treated him so well. He was a good dad."

I smiled with Mum as she reminisced. Her smile quickly turned into an expression I couldn't read, as she sighed heavily.

"What a wasted life. Why couldn't he be the good version of himself the full time? There was so much wasted time." She sobbed again, grieving the childhood that she should have had, and the man that my grandpa could have been. I squeezed her tightly as tears streamed down both our cheeks.

"I've told you before, that's why I left home for good at nineteen. To get away from the situation. That's why I moved from Oxford to Glasgow without knowing a soul. And that's why your uncle went to the army. We needed to get away. But he endured horrific things in the army – he saw things that no young boy should ever see."

As teenagers, my mum's brother, my uncle, was the first to leave home and go to the army. Recently, he'd spoken to us about his PTSD – how he struggled with flashbacks and anxiety. I've always thought what a shame his situation was – his only escape from childhood trauma was to endure even more trauma through the army. My mum said he even got put in army jail once. He ran away from the army before his contract ended; he needed to go home and help Granny when Grandpa was on a bad bender.

I was proud of my mum for starting a new life, here in Scotland. It's here where her world felt lighter. She made friends, enjoyed her work life, and even met my dad. It wasn't long until the darkness crept up on her again. A few years after her big move, Granny and Grandpa moved to Scotland too. As much as she would have been happy to see them again, when things got bad with Grandpa's drinking, I imagine she would have felt like that helpless little girl all over again, but this time with crushing responsibilities and shame. Mum told me how she took my granny to Women's Aid and helped her finally divorce my grandpa. Apparently, Grandpa always blamed my mum for this. When they split, Grandpa tried to kill himself. Thankfully, Mum found him, and he survived. In the years that followed, Grandpa got the help he needed and started attending AA meetings. He got clean and never touched alcohol again – this was a condition from my granny; otherwise, she wouldn't have taken him back.

I had such a sheltered, happy upbringing. I had no idea quite how dark and completely opposite my mum's childhood was to mine.

"Your grandpa tried so hard to stop drinking. It was hard for him. But he had to do it. Alcohol turned him into a completely different person – someone that none of us recognised. When he had a drink, something switched. It wasn't the real him."

"I'm so glad I've never seen that side of him. I can't believe how bad it was for you, Mum. I'm so sorry."

"Thanks, darling. He was such a good grandpa to you girls your whole life. He was absolutely wonderful to you both. I'd like to think that was his way of making up for all those bad years."

In the weeks thereafter, I contemplated the idea of second chances. My grandpa was given a second chance, and he made sure to use it wisely. I realised that people really could change – in a huge way. Although it's difficult, especially if addiction is a factor, it's not impossible. I realised that my grandpa's second chance wouldn't have been possible if it wasn't for his family's forgiveness. Secretly, forgiveness was something I couldn't give just yet. I needed time to process. Nonetheless, I could not imagine my grandpa as the old him. When I did, an unexpected emotion crept up on me. Anger. Anger and resentment towards my grandpa, for the first time in my life. I imagined my mum as a child and felt fiercely protective of her and furious for her. I carried that hurt heavily on my chest for several weeks. But then guilt would overrule. How could I possibly feel anger towards the man who boasts about me to the care home staff and spends hours playing chess with me? How could I possibly feel anger towards the man who made me laugh every time he saw me? How could I possibly feel anger towards my thoughtful, lovely grandpa? How could I possibly feel anger towards the man on his deathbed? I loved him so much. These mixed emotions were difficult to wrap my head around. I now understood why mum kept quiet for so long. She didn't want me to see him differently, but it was too late. Despite this, I'm so glad she told me. The truth is always important, no matter how hard a pill it is to swallow sometimes.

There was one part of me who saw my grandpa as his same, old self, but there was another side of me who couldn't look at him in the same way. It was so confusing to contemplate, especially when I would visit him in the care home, when I'd help care for him and see a vulnerable side to him.

As more time passed, my mental load lightened. I think that working in the prison played a huge part in that. I knew that if I continued to carry that resentment around with me, it would go against everything I stood for. I always talked about forgiveness, rehabilitation and second chances. Now it was my time to walk the walk. I knew, deep down, that people were more than the worst thing they ever did. My grandpa was more than the worst thing he ever did – so much more. He impacted my life in the most positive way. My life was better because of him, and if he was never given a second chance? I, and many others, would have missed out on that. My grandpa was a good person for as long as I could remember, for my entire life. Maybe there's no such thing as being a good person or being a bad person. Maybe we're all just humans who make varied extremities of good and bad choices.

I decided that I could let it go. Well, I could try. Seeing the love that my mum had for Grandpa really helped. After all, it was her that saw my grandpa at his worst – not me. If she could forgive him, then so could I. Of course, Grandpa never knew that I was feeling this way, and at that, I'm relieved.

Any lingering bitterness towards my grandpa for his past left me immediately on the day that he died. He passed away at hospital, in his sleep, hopefully peacefully. We made it there just after he took his last breath. My sister got there first – thankfully, she was with him in the moments before he passed. I'm so glad that she was there, holding his hand and talking with him. I'm so glad he wasn't alone. When I saw him, I felt an all-consuming feeling of not only grief, but of unconditional love and forgiveness. Seeing him on his deathbed changed me. Looking at him and knowing we would never see him again, knowing he'd never see us again, and not only that – he'd never see the world again. That was it for him. Something about his death felt so cruel and painful. The reality of it felt like a punch in the gut.

Now, we celebrate his life in small ways. Whenever "I Love It" by Icona Pop comes on the radio, I get a little teary, but I belt the song at the top of my lungs, just like my grandpa did. I have a "Mind Over Matter" print framed in my bedroom; I repeat the mantra when I need to, to help me overcome challenges, and when I do, I think of my grandpa cheering me on.

This experience has shaped how I view the prisoners that I've worked with. Prior to this, if you were to introduce me to a prisoner who was incarcerated for a domestic-related crime, I would have struggled to look beyond the things that they had done. I would have struggled to believe that they could change and be a good person. But now I've seen it for myself. I've not only seen it, but you could also say I've lived it in some way. It's been a personal experience. I'm not saying this to excuse and validate domestic abuse; I understand that it's not one size fits all. Don't get me wrong, I know there's many people out there who absolutely do not deserve a second chance, under any circumstances. However, I know there will be people out there like my grandpa, and from my experience, the good souls like that are usually worth forgiveness.

23

Case Study

I had three days off work after my grandpa passed. I probably should have taken longer, as I couldn't talk about him without tearing up. But I wanted to return sooner rather than later; I knew that being back at work would help me handle the grief better. When I was feeling low, sometimes I'd trick myself into feeling better. Alter-ego Teacher Aimee slapped a smile on and put on a show. I thought that if I pretended to be OK, I'd eventually feel OK. This kind of worked, but I still wasn't my same old self for a while. Fortunately, the boys at the prison made me laugh and feel better as usual; it was a form of escapism.

After some taster sessions, our new recruits settled in well. However, consistent attendance was still quite flaky. We went through a rough patch where Brandy was the only one to come down. We used the time well; we were able to put him through a few different qualifications, so we got the paperwork done for those. On another occasion, we used the time to interview Brandy for a case study. The case study would then be sent to our funders, showing how beneficial the dance project was in reducing crime and antisocial behaviour.

The day we interviewed Brandon reminded me of why we do what we do. We began the session in our usual way, making small talk about what was on TV. Brandy also gave us the inside scoop on prison gossip. Sam had gone to the bathroom and then stopped to talk with the prison officer on shift. So, it was just Brandy and I for a while. Sam used the time to make a recruitment action plan with the officer; we couldn't continue the sessions if only Brandy would show up each week.

"Brandy, I find it odd that we can't get more people down. I mean, you seem like a very well-liked person in here. I don't get why the others don't follow suit if they look up to you?"

Brandy looked puzzled himself. He shrugged his shoulders in agreement. "They try to tell me coming down to dance is gay, but I don't care what they think. I like it. I tell them, 'Get yourself fuckin' doon here and try it. It's only a bit of cardio, and it's also a decent laugh.' Anyway, it's not about what they think; it's about what a think, and a enjoy it."

I was relieved that Brandy felt this way. I was worried he'd feel put off because of the others. "Well, if you enjoy it so much, you won't mind doing us a favour. We've been asked to choose a participant to interview for a case study. Someone who we think has made positive change during their time with us, we think you'd be perfect."

"So, this goes to the funders? The people who have the power to keep these classes going?"

"Yep, that's right. Also, it's totally anonymous. Your name isn't used so no one knows it's you we are writing about."

"Aye, that's fine. I'll give ye all the right answers. Don't you worry."

"No, there's no such thing as a right answer. Just be honest."

"I'll be honest, aye. But the way a see it is, we need to say the right things so they keep funding the classes. I want the classes to keep going, so I'll be honest… with a few sprinkles on top."

I laughed away and tried my best to reiterate that there was no right or wrong. He finally accepted this idea, reluctantly so, and with that we began our interview. By this point, Sam and the prison officer came over and sat beside us. The officer wouldn't usually get involved; it wasn't ideal that his chosen time was now. I was worried that Brandy would hold back with his answers.

"OK, so the first question asks what your life was like before you joined our dance group."

Brandy put on his best well-spoken voice. He cleared his throat before speaking. He then rounded each word perfectly and slowly.

"I used to sit in the gaff, oot ma nut…" He paused before correcting himself. "Sorry, under the influence. I used to sit in my gaff, under the influence, with no drive to do anything. I would rather spend my Tuesday morning in my bed, until Sam and Aimee came along."

The more he spoke, the more softly spoken and polite he would sound. Brandy really knew how to put on a show. I went on to ask a bunch of questions, all to do with his achievements, turning points and challenges that he faced since starting the dance project. He spoke about how he enjoyed performing in front of an audience and working as part of a team. Not only did he get this experience through dance classes, but he also took drama and music lessons in the prison.

"What would you like to do when you get released from prison?"

"Panto!"

I couldn't tell if he was being serious. I could believe this to be true – I'd seen him in a few prison drama productions, and he was fantastic. I just couldn't tell because you never knew with Brandy; sarcasm was his thing.

"Really?" I asked, hoping he wouldn't see my question as a vote of no confidence.

"Aye, gen up. A was fuckin' born for panto!"

I had no idea what "gen up" meant, but I didn't want to interrupt.

"*Oh no you don't! Oh yes you can!*" Brandy chanted in his best over-animated panto voice.

"I can see it now," Sam said while laughing; we all were.

"What does 'gen up' mean?" I asked with slight reluctance. I normally knew all the young people lingo. I was one of the young people. Or so I thought.

"Gen up? You've no' heard of that? It just means 'genuinely' or 'really'."

"Ahh, I guessed as much but wasn't sure." I suddenly felt old.

"Aye, anyway, a need to be careful at the next panto. Last time, a mad granny in the audience had the hots for me. A wis scared."

The prison officer and Sam chatted amongst themselves as I finished asking Brandy the case study questions. It was a little difficult as he'd get distracted through overhearing their conversation. Lesson learnt: all case studies in private from now on. For the last question, I asked how his behaviour had changed for the better since joining our dance group.

"When I used to get mad, I'd want to box. Now, instead, I want a dance battle – *Step up 2*-style!" Brandy got up from his chair and showed his signature party move – the worm.

"As much as I love that for you, I'm not sure I believe you."

"OK, a get it. A need to gee yees an answer you can write in that notepad of yours. Well… I finally made it to the open hall, after two years of trying." Brandy edged towards his chair, breathless.

"Aw really?! Well in! What do you need to do to get moved there? Good behaviour?" I asked.

"Aye. Squeaky clean."

I felt a surge of pride. "Brandon, do you remember what you were like when you first started with us? Look at you now. Being moved to the open hall is such an achievement. Look how far you've come. I'm proud of you!"

I gave him a high five but instantly regretted it. I worried I was coming across as uncool and cringe. First the "gen up" fiasco and now this! My mental chatter came to a halt when I realised how absurd it was to give this much concern over how a participant viewed me. I came to my senses and relaxed. I really did mean it though; I was proud of him. The open hall was a hall where every prisoner wanted to be. It meant less time in their small cells and more time in the hall. There was more freedom. More freedom meant more trust. I instantly thought back to the days that Brandy would come to our class with a black eye from the fights he'd get into. It felt as though he was a different person now. That seemed so long ago. I also thought about his panto comment. I can confirm that Brandon was a natural showman. I had seen him in several prison drama shows, and I was always blown away, not just by him as an individual but by the whole production. The shows always covered such meaningful topics while also making the audience laugh. During the most recent show, my stomach hurt from laughing and my cheeks hurt from smiling.

Another audience member had turned to me and said, "This is hilarious. I could see this in the Edinburgh Fringe. It's good enough for sure!"

I had completely agreed. It wasn't just the comedy I favoured; it was the topics covered too. In the most recent show, the play explored how young people are judged harshly in society, as well as how much pressure young people face nowadays. They portrayed this in an entertaining yet clever way. They left the audience feeling hopeful, positive, and inspired. By the end of the performance, there was a buzz in the air. I could see how much it meant to the boys and how accomplished and worthy they felt. There's power in that. This value was not limited to the performers. They moved the audience. They changed perspectives. They challenged beliefs. They did something important. They provided a meaningful service. I feel that this was their contribution to society.

24

The New Recruits

Despite the unfortunate start to the taster sessions, we eventually led some which turned out well, and we got even more new recruits, enough to fill a brand-new class. Callum and Jordan were the most dedicated newbies. Their bond reminded me of Ant and Dec from *Britain's Got Talent*. Callum was short, around 5'5" or so, with thick, curly, brown hair and piercing blue eyes. Jordan was the total opposite – well over six feet tall, with thin, jet-black hair and deep-brown eyes. Callum was the chatty, computer whiz type, while Jordan was the cool, quiet, and aloof one. An unlikely pairing, but they bounced off one another so well.

As the months went on, they were a staple part of the group. At times, it felt as though they were the glue, especially Callum. If someone missed a session, Callum would go out of his way to spend time with them in the hall to catch them up. This was especially important because we were putting the participants through a dance leadership award, so lots of written work was involved. As I got to know him, it made more sense as to why he'd naturally take on this role. He was the pass man for performing arts. This meant that performing arts was part of his work party in the prison. He'd work closely with the performing arts officer to look after the space we'd use. This work involved cleaning and rearranging furniture, the sound system, technology, props, and instruments. He'd also try to recruit and support new participants.

We were a few weeks into the leadership course, and I made a comment about how I was losing my patience with the participants who were a no-show.

Callum jokingly replied with, "I could say the same about you!" His silly tone was one which was saved for those whom he favoured. I was off work, unwell, two weeks prior, so he was poking fun at that. This was his usual humour. I'd noticed how his banter had become more and more prominent with those he felt comfortable enough to let in. Later in the class during our check-in, I'd ask everyone to say how they were feeling that day, one at a time. When it got to Callum's turn, he'd respond sarcastically with, "I'm just happy to be here," in his mocking, softly spoken voice. This soon became a catchphrase of his. It was all in good nature. Jordan, on the other hand, kept himself to himself. He wasn't really the jokey type, unless he was joking with Callum; that's when he'd let loose.

One afternoon in October, we were teaching the group a Halloween dance. Jordan was being lifted high into the air by the others, with his hands crossed over his chest as if he was a mummy in a coffin. His stomach faced the sky, his back faced the floor, and he was in a laid-down position. I had to help with lifting him due to a few participants being off. It was going well. Michael Jackson's "Thriller" blared through the speakers, Sam was calling out instructions, so we safely executed the lift. Jordan was smiling from ear to ear and telling us what a buzz it was to be lifted so high.

Then out of nowhere… "Aghhhhh!"

We panicked and put him down at lightning speed.

"What? What is it?" Sam queried with utter confusion.

"It was Aimee! She stabbed me."

I was baffled. Then I looked down at my nails and remembered they were pointy acrylics! I didn't know what to say

"Oh no! I am so sorry! That was an accident, I promise."

I was met with silence. Thankfully, an outbreak of laughter followed, and I realised I was off the hook. Thank goodness for that; the last thing I needed was to make an enemy in the prison. Jordan never let me live it down. For the next few months, he'd find a way to slip it into every possible conversation as a joke. With that, he started to slowly come out of his shell.

A few weeks later, it was International Women's Day. A member of the youth work team dropped by to performing arts and handed a certificate to both me and Sam. On each certificate, it read, "To celebrate International Women's Day, you have been nominated for giving us something to look forward to each week and for being a good person." It made my day. We later found out that Callum nominated us and organised the full thing, as we expected. I remember feeling so happy that we had made such a positive impact. This meaningful influence became more apparent in conversation with Callum during tea break that afternoon. We were collecting quotes from all participants to add to our end-of-term report, which was submitted to the funders of the project every few months. When interviewing Callum, his answer was beyond our expectations. For once, he spoke in a serious manner, without his usual mocking and teasing tone.

"I've dealt with depression and anxiety my whole life, and I cope with it relatively well. But performing arts has played a major part in helping me with it since I've been in here. I don't know how I'd cope in here without it. I want to continue with performing arts when I leave prison. It's not only the endorphins we get which makes dance so beneficial, but it's also having responsibility and routine." He seemed sincere and honest.

Later that day, Callum revealed that he was working hard on a music project – writing and recording his own songs. He explained how he valued our opinions and how he'd like us to give it a listen and let him know our thoughts.

"You guys are the closest thing I've got to anyone on the outside at the moment."

That comment touched me. I wanted to leave the young people better off than how I found them. Even with a small act of kindness through supporting them through their goals and providing encouragement, this was enough to make a positive difference. Callum handed over a CD. His full name was scribbled in black ink over its case. Seeing this CD made me feel incredibly nostalgic. I was instantly transported back in time; fourteen-year-old me had a weekly hobby which consisted of making new dance playlists and burning them to blank CDs. This was before Spotify or Apple Music were a thing.

As we got on with the class, Callum and Jordan entertained us with their creative duet. Sam was trying some tricky development tasks with the group. She asked them to be open-minded and to try some tasks which would make them feel out of their comfort zones. Although there was some resistance at first, we managed to win them over.

"Guys, the more you try these things that seem daunting, the braver and more open you will become in general. These experiences are shaping you. In the future, when you are given the opportunity to try new things to better yourself, you will be more likely to take that risk, because you'll think back to these experiences in performing arts."

I babbled on, and with that there was no more resistance… they probably just wanted to shut me up! To be fair, the defiance never came from Callum and Jordan; they just got on with it. In fact, they were loving it by the end. Sam had everyone in partners. Partner A had to close their eyes and Partner B had to guide them around the room, manipulating their movement. This task made the participants feel vulnerable, so it required a lot of trust. That's why Jordan and Callum coped so well; they already had this faith and support between them. I was stunned. Sam had them trying creative tasks which we'd usually only try with more advanced dance college students. They were such a good group. As the improvisation went on, Sam encouraged them to visualise paint all over their bodies. She asked them how they'd use their different body parts to make paintings in the air or on the floor.

"How did you find that?" Sam asked when it was over.

There were a few cheerful mumbles and comments overall.

"You really enjoyed it, didn't you?" Sam shot a smug look Jordan's way.

He wore a huge smile across his face, which was rare. The only other time I had noticed it was during our Halloween dance… and we all know how that turned out.

Jordan responded gleefully, "Yeah! I was the paint and Callum was the brush."

Soon enough, we were able to put our new class through their Award in Dance Leadership. This involved a lot of written work, as well as the practical side of things. We taught the boys about leadership skills such as communication, motivation, organisation, and teamwork. They eventually worked their way up to teaching one another. They had to prepare a warm-up, a game and a dance sequence to teach; they did this with a partner on several occasions. It wasn't easy for the group, but it was an enjoyable challenge. They seemed to understand how transferrable these leadership skills were, so much so that one participant stated, "I'm never gonna be a dancer, but I want to be a painter and decorator when I get out. One day, I'm gonna need to teach someone else how to paint a wall. This course has helped with my ability to do that." The guys really surprised us with their music and dance style choices. We had some teach salsa dance (well, their version of salsa!). We had others use "Get'cha Head in the Game" from the *High School Musical* soundtrack. We even had one participant try his hand at Bollywood. It was a safe space for these young men to let out their silly, curious, childlike sides. When these prisoners were actual children, from what many of them had told me, they didn't have the opportunity to act in this way. Instead, they were trying to be the big man, trying to look and act cool. Trying to fit in, rather than trying to belong. In our dance space, they were allowed to experiment and try new things. It was a place of no judgement. Instead, it was a place of laughter, curiosity, and fun.

Once all the participants had achieved their dance leadership awards, we organised an end-of-term show where we could invite a small audience, mostly other workers from the prison, youth work, or local performing arts companies. On the lead-up to the performance, Jordan was really coming into his own. I usually couldn't imagine him without his other half, Callum. But in the last few rehearsals, I'd noticed he was independently putting himself out there a bit more. On our last rehearsal for our contemporary dance, he even went barefoot! That's how professional contemporary dancers perform. Up until that moment, I never would have imagined a young man in the prison embracing this professional dance etiquette.

Callum was also doing well, as usual. He was always up the front with other boys watching him as they danced, relying on him for timing cues. I had to tell him to stop looking at the floor so much. It didn't add up: he was one of the most competent dancers in the class; he should have had way more confidence.

The performance went well. They showed off their street dance and contemporary routines. You could tell they got such a buzz from performing in front of an audience. I felt strangely nervous for them right before they went on. I really wanted them to feel proud of themselves and for it to all go to plan. It was at that moment I realised just how much I cared about this group and how much I was going to miss them. I had been asked to teach on a new dance project which happened to run on the same day as the prison classes. With slight hesitation, I accepted the new project offer. I accepted with the hope of returning to the prison one day. The new project was a whole different ball game. I was being asked to teach cross-curricular dance in primary schools. The aim of the new project was to teach creative movement to reinforce classroom learning. I had little experience with this type of work; I had been teaching dance in prison on and off for around four years at that point. I knew which project was going to help me grow as a practitioner and learn more. Nevertheless, it didn't make the decision any easier.

After the group had danced, we called them out one at a time to receive their dance leadership certificates. The audience cheered loudly in support of every participant. Their warm smiles showed just how much this meant to them. Jordan even gave me a hug. The audience gave wonderful feedback, which offered the boys another boost of accomplishment. From there, everyone mingled and helped themselves to the range of snacks that Sam and I provided. There seemed to be queues of people lined up to speak to the performers. They must have felt like celebrities.

When the audience finally left, Sam handed me a card which was signed by the full group. She must have told them that I was leaving and sneakily got them to sign it while I was preoccupied. It was so thoughtful and really made my decision to leave even more difficult. In the card, there was a range of sweet and funny messages:

Thank you for teaching me. It means a lot. You are good energy to be around.

Thanks for a year of laughs and making my time go by faster. Good luck for the future.

Cheers for always having a smile and trying to get everyone smiling as well, good luck!

Thanks so much for your support. You are the best. Wishing you all the best.

I'm glad I put in the time and sweat to become a dance leader. Now I can cut shapes like a god in the club. Thanks.

Thanks for putting up with our unorthodox dance group.

I was blown away with the kind messages, but my last day wasn't over yet. After lunch, it was time for Brandy's group to shine, the group we had been working with for the longest.

25

The Return of *Magic Mike*

Sam and I took the long walk from performing arts to the reception desk. We handed in our visitor passes to the prison officer on shift and explained we'd be back after lunch. Once I got to my car, I lifted my phone from my bag and noticed a text from my gran, asking how I was doing today. I replied with, *At the prison today, loving it!* I laughed to myself as I re-read my message, realising how bizarre and comical that sentence would sound to most.

We hit up our usual spot for lunch, our good old café! Sam and I chatted away about the success of the day so far, as well as catching up on each other's lives outside of work. We even had time for me to run lesson-plan ideas by Sam and get her feedback. I was going to miss this. Sam had become such a good friend, a work big sister even. I had learnt so much from collaborating with her; she had been in the job for around fifteen years! I felt lucky to work with her.

After picking up extra snacks for the afternoon performance, we headed back to the prison. We had a full list of snacks that the prisoners requested – from McDonald's to hummus, we'd heard it all! Many of their requests were bizarre. In the end, we opted for cupcakes and biscuits. When we re-entered the prison, we handed over our IDs in exchange for our visitor passes, put our food in the conveyer belt and walked through the body scanner. While doing so, I felt slightly uneasy, so I gave my best *I-promise-I'm-not-smuggling-drugs-in* smile as the food slid through the other side of the scanner.

When we arrived at performing arts, I reluctantly informed the group of my decision to leave so I could take on a new project. They mostly seemed happy for me and asked lots of questions about the type of work I'd be doing.

"Nah, not good enough. Abandoning us," Brandy interrupted in a light-hearted manner while half smiling.

"No, not at all. This was a hard decision for me to make. Sam will still be here," I responded pleadingly.

"Only half the team coming back…" Brandy paused before continuing, as if trying to create dramatic effect. "So only half as good." Brandy carried an insolent smile alongside a judgemental shrug while Sam berated him for his comments.

After well-needed rehearsal time, the audience arrived at the performing-arts space and the show began. That tingly nervy feeling sat in my stomach once again as I watched the group give it their best effort. The dance was a mash-up of assorted styles alongside creative movement which the boys had choreographed. It was based on the mind map question that we set months ago: "Who do I want to be?" The piece started with a drill track and all the boys sitting on chairs. Each dancer performed their own short solo, based on their personality traits. Some dancers took on a more serious approach to their movement while others showed off their witty side. One boy faced the back of the room and wrapped his arms around his torso, so we could see his hands on his back as he swayed side to side, mimicking kissing someone passionately. Another boy stood up on his chair and showed sharp, punchy movements while flexing his biceps. One participant slouched far back on his chair, demonstrating heavy, lethargic movement. Maybe this was to convey his lazy side, or maybe he was showing his lack of motivation since being incarcerated.

The boys travelled to their duet partners and showed off their strength and co-ordination through a range of lifts and tricks. At this part I heard a few gasps from the audience. There were also a few claps and high pitched "woos" in support for this exciting part of the performance. From there, the music changed twice more for the hip hop and contemporary sections of the dance. To end the piece, the boys walked back to their chairs from the start and stood on top of them, in the same way we'd rehearsed many times before.

But then something unexpected happened. Brandy whipped his t-shirt off! My jaw almost hit the floor. Then the rest of the boys took their t-shirts off, one at a time in a Mexican wave pattern. They all had big writing in black ink on their abdomens as well as curved lines down their stomachs, creating the illusion of a six-pack! Each prisoner wore one letter, so when standing together their letters created a word. The word they'd made was the name of the dance company that Sam and I worked for. I couldn't believe it. This was both sweet yet slightly disturbing… I could see myself being scouted to choreograph for Diamond Dolls strip club if they kept this up!

Once the performance was over and the boys received a huge cheer, I found myself announcing, "We didn't choreograph that last part; it was all them! Sam and I knew nothing about it, I swear!"

The audience's laughter eased my slight concern, and I was able to laugh alongside them. I was having flashbacks to Brandy 's very first day, how he stripped off and whipped his t-shirt round like a lasso. I remembered how much he irritated me that day and how I'd secretly hoped I wouldn't see him again. How wrong was I? Well, in my defence, he was tuned to the moon that day. Thankfully, I had never seen him in that state since.

Once the boys received their certificates and another big cheer from the audience, Sam facilitated a Q&A so we could note down some useful quotes for our funders. There were so many positive comments from the audience, praising their confidence, their teamwork, and their skill execution. We then asked the prisoners some questions. Sam read each question through the mic. She then handed the mic to whoever raised their hand to answer. Last week, we gave the boys a heads-up of what the questions would be, so they didn't feel put on the spot. Here are some of the recordings from our Q&A:

"What do you like about the dance classes we teach?"

"I love dance because it's fun and entertaining and the staff are nice and friendly. I also love the way they teach us new styles of dance."

"The dance classes take my mind off everything… I might even continue with dance when I get out."

"It's fun, and you guys are friendly. I enjoy everything."

"It's a good laugh… I've built more confidence inside and outside the dance class, social confidence. I enjoy the games because of the teamwork aspect."

"I enjoyed when we got to perform in the showcase; it was a nice way to wrap it all together."

"It's so much more than dancing. It's becoming fit and healthy, it's working together as a team, it's literacy skills, it's being creative."

"What was your favourite part of the course?"

"Having a laugh, getting out the gaff and getting fit!"

"Challenging myself with the dance leadership assessments. I enjoyed learning how to put all the leadership skills we were taught into practice through teaching the other guys."

"Being part of a team with these guys!"

"What was your biggest achievement on the course?"

"Gaining the dance leadership qualification."

"Sticking at something consistently."

"What would you change about the course?"

"I wish that you came into the prison more often. Look at what we've achieved with you coming in once a week; imagine what we could do if you were here a few times a week."

That last comment was a perfect way to end the discussion, and a perfect way to end my time with the group. I felt a huge wave of pride, fulfilment, and purpose. I hoped the boys felt the same. The mingling part of the afternoon commenced, everyone enjoyed the refreshments and chatted amongst themselves. I chatted to a few of the prisoners while helping myself to snacks.

"Do yous not think it's such a shame that some of the guys missed the performance today? Why have they not been turning up?" In all honesty, it wasn't that deep. The boys who were absent had only joined a few weeks ago and I could tell their hearts weren't in it. We hadn't quite won them over yet. But still, I was curious.

"The harsh truth is, they're all stoned. They'd rather be stoned oot their nuts than doing something productive with their time," Brandon stated frankly while tutting disapprovingly. To my surprise, there was no undertone of sarcasm or quick wit, not in the slightest. Brandy's condemnation was deadly serious for once.

I couldn't help but chuckle in response. "Brandon, do you remember what you were like on your first day of dance class?"

Brandon turned to the other boys who weren't incarcerated at the time. "I turned up absolutely fucked," he said with a slight laugh.

"Yep, you did," I agreed. "He was being a bad role model for the rest of the class. Instead of joining in, he was stripping and waving his t-shirt in the air, distracting the rest of the group," I explained as I gave a visual interpretation of swinging an imaginary t-shirt in circles above my head.

The others smiled in response. They were then pulled away by eager members of the audience who wanted a piece of them. Brandon remained occupied in our conversation.

"I'll be honest, Brandon, my first thought back then was how I didn't want to see you again. I can't believe the change in you."

Luckily, Brandon took this in the way it was intended. He reflected on how far he'd come as a person. He had truly come full circle.

"Aye, well look at us now! I'm your favourite now, aren't a?"

"I don't have any favourites!" I chimed back while laughing as he flashed a cheeky wink my way.

"Do you think I could get a job as a dance instructor when I get out?" he asked half jokingly, half serious.

Before I could respond, he described all the leadership skills he had learnt and improved upon through his time at the dance project. At the end of his sentence, he motioned the action of a mic drop.

"I don't see why not." I paused to sip my tea. "I'm always searching for new ways that we could support young men once they're released from prison. That would be amazing, so who knows!"

In all honesty, this is something that I'd been thinking of for a while. I just wasn't sure how the ex-prisoners would get round the strict background checks. It was going to be difficult and out of my control. This frustrated me. I wanted to give opportunities for a fresh start, for a second chance. How could I do this? I didn't have the answers. All I had was hope. I didn't share any of these concerns with Brandon, not wanting to bring him down from his natural high. Instead, I changed the subject.

"Where's your band gone?" For the last few months, I noticed he wasn't wearing the wristband which held a photograph of his mum who'd passed away almost ten years prior. He must have only been around ten or eleven when she died. The thought of this made my stomach sink and my heart heavy. I suddenly felt incredibly ditzy for changing the subject to something so sad when the attempt was to keep his buzz going. It was just the first thing I could think of to say, and I was genuinely curious.

"A keep it in ma gaff now 'cause it broke. Don't wanna risk losing it; that's a few times that's almost happened. I also have a different chain with my mum's ashes in it. When I thought I'd lost that one time, I went mental. A wis pounding the streets of ma scheme looking for it. A was in a rage with everyone a passed and getting up to all sorts that day. When I got searched by the police that day, a eventually found it. Guess where it wis after all that? It had fell doon tae the bottom of ma t-shirt."

The conversation eventually circulated back to the prison dance group. Brandy revealed to Sam that he'd been trying to recruit new members. He went on to say this was especially important now that the performance was over and they'd be starting a fresh theme and new choreography. It was the perfect time for newbies to join. I silently observed the conversation between Sam and Brandon, knowing I was no longer part of this. I had a major case of FOMO (Fear Of Missing Out), as the young people would say.

"Aye, I'll make them come along… I can be very convincing," Brandy proclaimed. Just when we thought he'd changed his ways.

"OK, but no threats!" Sam ordered.

"No promises," Brandy replied with a mischievous grin.

We didn't have time to say much else. It was time for the audience members to be escorted back to reception. Sam and I were asked to go with the group, otherwise we'd be waiting for another half hour before we'd be allowed to leave. We said our goodbyes quickly before leaving. The group wished me luck and offered up a knuckle punch. I even received a hug from Brandy. It was bittersweet, but I had a strong feeling that this wasn't the end of my time there. I'd be back. I'd go away, upskill, and return to the prison with a strengthened ability to make change.

There was more change to make. There was more to learn. There was more to give. There were more people to heal. There was more toxic masculinity to abolish. There were more perceptions to shift. There were more minds to open. There was more compassion to surrender. There was more rehabilitation to offer. There were more second chances to give.

26

What Is Your Call to Action?

This book is about young prisoners, yes, but this book is also about you. It's about me. It's about all of us. It's about: trauma, Adverse Childhood Experiences, addiction, well-being, tacit assumptions, gender stereotypes, toxic masculinity, neglect and loneliness, emotional intelligence, homelessness, our school system, identity, our innate desire to belong and connect with others, and so much more. These are things which can affect everyone. Therefore, this isn't a book merely about prisoners. It's a book about our society. These issues don't only affect incarcerated people. For most, these problems don't lead to incarceration. However, there is impact, nonetheless. Whether that's in the form of poor health, broken homes, poverty, financial setbacks, relationship hardships, abuse, anger issues, mental health problems, or even in the form of mindset and personality difficulties.

As a society, we are the cause but we're also the solution. Everyone has a role to play. Whether you're the school teacher or the school janitor. Whether you're the social worker or the family friend. Whether you're the social media influencer or the quiet neighbour across the road. No matter how big or small your role is in the lives of others, don't take it lightly. Especially if you have a role in the lives of children.

What is your call to action?

Can you stand up for what's right?

When you hear discriminative language, stereotypes, or assumptions, could you challenge it? Could you educate others instead of staying quiet? Could you educate yourself?

Could you be an advocate for those who you suspect to live in abusive households? Even if it's not your place. Well, who's place is it, exactly?

Can you forgive?

If you're an employer, could you give an ex-prisoner a job? Could you give someone that second chance?

Could you donate money to homeless shelters or mental health charities?

Could you sign a petition to increase the funding given to free community arts programmes?

Could you offer words of encouragement to someone who needs it?

If you have a role in the lives of young people, could you teach them about mental well-being? About self-love? About emotional intelligence? About not judging others? About what it means to have a moral compass?

Spoiler: it's not just children who need to learn these things; we're all a work in progress.

27

Epilogue

One year later, I was back regularly teaching at the prison again. My instincts were right. I learnt a lot during my time away, so I knew I'd made the right decision taking on the new project. When I returned, I saw some familiar faces, such as Mr Magic Mike himself. Brandy was doing well and had utilised his leadership skills to take on an assisting role in some of the protection classes. He even became the pass man of performing arts. This meant that helping at performing arts was part of his work party, so he was based down there, working for the performing arts prison officer, to get some extra cash.

Many lads from the old cohort had moved to a new prison or had finished their sentences. Callum's circumstance was the latter, and so he was released. Shortly after, I bumped into him at a restaurant in Glasgow city centre. It had been well over a year since I'd last saw him, so when I clocked him, I couldn't be sure it was definitely him. He looked quite different. I think his hair and beard were styled differently, so it threw me off, that, and the fact he was no longer wearing prison attire. Nonetheless, I plucked up the courage to say hello. He seemed both pleased and surprised to see me, so after giving me a hug, he updated me on how well he was doing since being released. He was still in touch with his sidekick – big tall Jordan, the one I accidently stabbed with my acrylic nails. Callum said that Jordan was well, now at a different jail, closer to his family so he could get more regular visits. Callum said he had a job, a girlfriend and decent pals to hang out with at the weekend. His life seemed good. I was so glad.

After one year of being back at the prison, I decided that it was time to leave the dance world behind and try my hand at a career change. At this point, I had worked for the same dance company since leaving college – for six years. I loved it, but I was ready for a new challenge. For such a long time, I had worked in the prison and wondered if something could have been done sooner to prevent these young men from being incarcerated in the first place. I wanted to make a difference before it was too late. So, I decided to go back to uni and study primary school teaching. Thankfully, I already had a degree in dance, so I could take on the post-graduate course, qualifying after just one year.

As I write the final words of this book, I have completed my uni course and I'm preparing to have my own wee class. I'm so excited. I can't wait to have my own class that I teach and look after every single day. While working as a dance teacher, I often noticed the positive impact that I had on my students, even when I only saw them once a week. I can only imagine the positive difference I could make after seeing my pupils all day, every day.

Recently, I was invited back to a school that I was based at for my first placement at uni. It was a P7 class, and I was asked back to attend their leavers' prom. As I entered the gym hall, I was instantly greeted with so many cuddles. They were so excited to see me. I couldn't believe it; I had only known them for five weeks and had last seen them around six months prior. I didn't expect all the commotion. Small groups of them chatted away with me and even asked for selfies with me. It was a wholesome night. At the end of the celebrations, the kids gathered outside to release balloons. While this happened, "The Climb" by Miley Cyrus played loudly on a speaker, as emotional parents gathered to take photos and cheer for their children. When the music stopped, parents approached their children for hugs and pictures. I noticed that one boy in the class didn't have any family around him. I gave it a few minutes. I then went over and asked where his parents were. He put on a brave face as he told me they weren't coming. I admired his resilience as he smiled and seemed untouched. However, I found it hard to believe that he wouldn't have been hurt by this, no matter how fine he seemed. Children are good at putting on masks. At that moment, I thought to myself, *this is it... this is the whole point. This is why I want to be a teacher.*

I replied with, "Well, I just came over to tell you how proud of you I am. You should be so proud of yourself! You've completed primary school – how fantastic! You're going to do amazing things in high school; I can just tell."

His face lit up as he thanked me. For some reason, that moment really touched me, and I felt a little emotional. I wonder if it touched him in the same way. I'm committed to being the teacher who cheers for all her pupils, especially the ones who have no one else cheering them on. I want to be someone who makes everyone feel like a someone. I want to be that teacher who says, "I believe in you, you can do this, I'm proud of you." Every child deserves to feel seen and loved. We don't know how many children aren't getting this at home, and we don't know the impact this could have. In other words, I want to be a real life Miss Honey – although I'm sure when some pupils have caught me on a bad day, they'd sooner recognise me as Miss Trunchbull! But hey, it's the thought that counts.

One day during my post-grad year at uni, when I got home from placement, I was chatting with my mum and told her about my day, teaching the class. I explained how I facilitated a well-being check-in to find out how each child was feeling. I told her how I made sure to follow up on it, having one-to-one chats with the children who needed it.

Her reply was, "Wow, that's amazing. No one ever did a check-in with me when I was at school. No one ever asked if I was OK. I wasn't."

I thought back to my mum's experiences as a child, dealing with her alcoholic, abusive dad – my grandpa. I was instantly reminded how important these check-ins were.

I believe that the experiences I've had in the prison have hugely contributed to the difference I'll make as a primary school teacher. I've learnt that all behaviour is communication – often, an emotional need not being met. Hearing stories from the prisoners about their childhoods has made me see any child that I'll teach going forwards through a different lens – through a cautious lens.

Every day, when my pupils enter the classroom, I will greet each one of them with enthusiasm and kindness. I will show them how glad I am to see them; I know not all children will get this acknowledgement at home. I will teach the children about consent and human rights – the boys in my care will understand that girls are not their property and that no means no. My classroom will celebrate diversity in religion, culture, ethnicity and gender. Through this, I hope to teach my pupils to be open-minded and empathetic, abolishing discrimination and prejudice. I don't want our next generation to be instigators or participants of hate crimes. I hope to teach my class how to cope with their emotions in healthy ways, so they don't grow up as adults getting into frequent fistfights, resulting in prison sentences, or worse. I want to raise young people who are unafraid to have meaningful conversations, to delve in and talk about their feelings. I want to give every child in my care a sense of belonging.

Speaking of belonging, for the first time, this is something that I now feel in a romantic capacity. I have a wonderful partner who treats me like a princess, making me feel so loved, seen and valued. I feel forever safe with him, and I can't wait to see what our future holds. He's also a primary school teacher – which has been handy during my intense year at uni. He's supported me through it in more ways than I could have ever imagined. I wish he could have met my grandpa; they would have got on so well. I can picture them playing chess together and bonding while watching the wrestling.

My grandpa's mind-over-matter mantra is what helped me write this book. As you know, I am not an experienced writer. A teacher, yes, but I have no training, experience or qualifications in writing a book. However, I have thoroughly enjoyed the process, and I can't believe I've been brass enough to give it a go. If I hadn't embodied the mind-over-matter mentality, then it wouldn't have been possible. I had to believe in myself and in this project fully to give it my all. If you're reading this, I hope this book has touched you in some way. No matter how big or small, I hope that this book has left a mark. If it wasn't for the forgiveness that my grandpa received, I wouldn't be here telling this story. So, this book is for him – and for anyone else who believes in second chances.

Acknowledgements

At the heart of this book are the two people it is dedicated to. Mum, thank you for having the courage to trust me with your stories. Your strength inspires me every single day. Granny, thank you for always seeing the best in people and for being the least judgemental person I have ever known. Thank you for being the first person to read this book all those years ago, when it was only a fraction of what it is now. Even then, you encouraged me endlessly and helped me believe that this book had a real chance of being published. Without your support and belief, I'm not sure I would have believed in myself enough to persevere.

I would also like to thank my twin sister, Mikhaila, for always rooting for me, for proofreading alongside me, for giving me great advice, and for showing such pride and enthusiasm for this book on my behalf.

Dad, when you told me you would be the first person in line to buy my book, it touched me more than you'll ever know. Thank you for the many life lessons you have taught me over the years and for your constant support.

To my darling Ceb, thank you for always being there for me. You are my safe place and my sunshine.

To the rest of my family and friends, you know who you are. I love you all so much.

Thank you to the entire team at The Book Guild, especially Rosie Lowe and Carolina Santos. You have made my first publishing journey such a fantastic experience. It has been a pleasure working with you all, and I hope to do so again in the future.

Additionally, I would like to thank everyone who has purchased a copy of this book and anyone who has supported my journey as a new author. I appreciate you more than I can say.

Perhaps most importantly, I would like to thank every single person I taught at the prison. Thank you for inspiring me to write this book and for sharing your stories with me. I am also deeply grateful to everyone I worked with during my time there, from the prison officers to the youth work team, and most notably, my dance teacher colleagues. I miss you all dearly and will always cherish our time working together.

You're Not Alone

Helplines and Support

Families Outside
Support for families and friends of prisoners in Scotland.
Helpline: 0800 254 0088

Nacro – Criminal Record Support Service
For criminal record advice and assistance post-release.
Phone: 0300 123 199
Email: helpline@nacro.org.uk

Scottish Domestic Abuse and Forced Marriage Helpline (run by Scottish Women's Aid)
Phone (24/7 free): 0800 027 1234
Text/WhatsApp: 07401 288 595
Email: helpline@sdafmh.org.uk

Shakti Women's Aid (Edinburgh, BME-specific)
Support for Black and Minority Ethnic women, children, and young people.
Phone: 0131 475 2399 Website: shaktiedinburgh.co.uk

Scottish Women's Rights Centre
Provides legal help and immigration-related advice.
Helpline: 0808 801 0789

Refuge
For women and children in the UK, who are suffering or at risk of suffering from domestic violence.
Helpline: 0808 2000 247

NHS 24 – Mental Health Services (Scotland)
Free listening, advice, and signposting for all ages.
Call: 111

Samaritans
Confidential 24/7 support line.
Phone: 116 123

SANEline
For those experiencing mental health challenges or supporting someone who is.
Phone: 0300 304 7000 (4:30pm–10pm daily)

CALM (Campaign Against Living Miserably)
Support for men facing suicidal thoughts.
Phone: 0800 58 58 58 (5pm–midnight daily)

Shout
The UK's free, confidential, 24/7 text-messaging service for anyone who is struggling to cope.
Text 'SHOUT' to 85258

SAMH (Scottish Action for Mental Health)
Scotland-wide support and advocacy for mental health.
Live web chat: https://www.samh.org.uk/find-help
Phone: 0344 800 0550

Alcoholics Anonymous (UK)
Peer-support meetings and helpline.
Freephone: 0800 917 7650
Email: help@aamail.org

Drinkline
Confidential helpline for concerns about drinking.
Phone: 0300 123 1110 (weekdays 9 am–8pm; weekends 11 am–4pm)

Scottish Families Affected by Alcohol & Drugs (SFAD)
Support for anyone affected by someone else's substance use.
Website: sfad.org.uk

We Are With You
Confidential support for alcohol, drug, and mental health challenges across Scotland.
website: wearewithyou.org.uk

Shelter Scotland
Free housing advice helpline.
Phone: 0808 800 4444 (Mon–Fri 9 am–5pm)

Scottish Refugee Council – Homelessness Support
Free advice line.
Phone: 0808 196 7274

Homeless Project Scotland

Volunteer-run services including a 24/7 phone line, soup kitchen, shelters, and street teams.

Website: https://homelessprojectscotland.org

Bibliography

Books & Academic Works

Brown, B. (2010) *The Gifts of Imperfection: Let Go of Who You Think You're Supposed to Be and Embrace Who You Are*. Center City, MN: Hazelden Publishing.

Byrne, R. (2006) *The Secret*. New York: Atria Books.

Doyle, G. (2020) *Untamed*. New York: The Dial Press.

Haine, S. (2019) *Trauma is Really Strange*. Bath: Trauma Recovery Centre.

Ratey, J.J. (2008) *Spark: The Revolutionary New Science of Exercise and the Brain*. New York: Little, Brown Spark.

Van der Kolk, B.A. (2015) *The Body Keeps the Score: Brain, Mind, and Body in the Healing of Trauma*. London: Penguin Books.

Reports & Studies

Public Health Wales (2015) Adverse Childhood Experiences (ACEs) in Wales: A National Survey Examining Their Prevalence and Impact on Health Behaviours. Cardiff:

Public Health Wales. Available at: https://phw.nhs.wales/files/aces/ace-report-e.pdf (Accessed: 30 August 2025).

Russek, L.G. and Schwartz, G.E. (1997) 'Feelings of parental caring predict health status in midlife: A 35-year follow-up of the Harvard Mastery of Stress Study', Journal of Behavioral Medicine, 20(1), pp. 1–13.

Podcasts & Media

Bagdonas, N. and Woodward, E. (2020) 'How Laughter Can Be the Best Medicine', *The Wellness Scoop* [Podcast].

Sprouts (2018) *The Attachment Theory: How Childhood Affects Life*. YouTube. Available at: https://www.youtube.com/watch?v=WjOowWxOXCg (Accessed: 30 August 2025).

Zeedyk, S. (2016) *Pre-Birth to Three*. YouTube, uploaded by Education Scotland. Available at: https://www.youtube.com/watch?v=2lyjNIIJ0LM (Accessed: 30 August 2025).

Organisations & Websites

Children in Scotland (2021) The Teenage Brain [Webinar].

Enlightened Recovery (n.d.) Enlightened Recovery Website. Available at: https://enlightenedrecovery.com (Accessed: 30 August 2025).

Process Recovery Center (n.d.) The Process Recovery Center Website. Available at: https://www.theprocessrecoverycenter.com (Accessed: 30 August 2025).

Shelter Scotland (2023) Homelessness Statistics. Available at: https://scotland.shelter.org.uk (Accessed: 30 August 2025).

About the author

Aimee Friel is an author and primary school teacher from Glasgow. As a former dance artist, she's worked with a wide range of groups – including schools, secure units, and parent-and-baby classes. She taught dance for several years at a prison – an experience that inspired her debut memoir. Aimee holds a BA (Hons) degree in Dance and a postgraduate degree in Education.